with best wishes
Colin Morris .

GLORY DAYS

Reading Transport

Colin Morris

Ian Allan
PUBLISHING

Front cover: Already marked up for its return journey to Wokingham Road on route 17, Sunbeam S7/ Park Royal 68-seater No 178 (ERD 149) of 1950 approaches the Bear Inn at Tilehurst. Notwithstanding a slightly askew drop-down window on the lower deck, this vehicle was one of three of its type to remain in service until the very last day. *Mike Hodges*

Back cover: En route to Shinfield Road on 6 April 1968, No 78 (GRD 578D), from the final batch of Dennis Loline IIIs, passes over High Bridge in Duke Street. Above are the trolleybus wires to Mill Lane depot; beneath the similarly bound tram rails. In March 1903 the Corporation had paid William Weeks £1 19s 0d (£1.95) to 'cut the crown' of the bridge, to get the trams over. *Mike Hodges*

Back cover (inset): The full achievement of the arms of the Borough of Reading, with added identifying scroll beneath, as carried latterly by Reading Transport vehicles, until the Local Government Act 1974 and the later legislation of 1985 made municipalities hide away such gaudy things. 'RE' is a thank-you to Elizabeth I, while the rams depict Reading's early dependence upon the woollen industry. Beautiful! Shame!

CONTENTS

For H. Edgar Jordan, pioneer Reading Transport historian

First published 2005
ISBN (10) 0 7110 3068 5
ISBN (13) 978 0 7110 3068 8

© Colin Morris 2005
Published by Ian Allan Publishing an imprint of Ian Allan Publishing Ltd, Hersham, Surrey KT12 4RG
Printed in England by Ian Allan Printing Ltd, Hersham, Surrey KT12 4RG
Code: 0511/B

Visit the Ian Allan Publishing website at www.ianallanpublishing.com

Title page: First numerically of the 1962 Dennis Loline III/ East Lancs double-deckers, No 29 (29 DP) departs the Stations on trolleybus-replacement service 16 to Whitley Wood. The type took up the task with effect from 9 January 1967. The availability of the Loline, a licence-built version of the Bristol Lodekka, allowed Reading gradually to dispense with its traditional lowbridge types. *Mike Hodges*

Left: Passing the Minster of St Mary-the-Virgin (founded 979) on Wednesday 10 April 1974 are two of Reading's famous 'standee' saloons. Bristol RELL6G No 280 (NDP 280G), *en route* from Stations to St Michael's, Tilehurst, leads AEC Reliance No 50 (5150 DP), which type had pioneered that route more than a decade previously. Henry VIII's destruction of Reading Abbey provided the stone for the beautifully chequered background. *Colin Morris*

ACKNOWLEDGEMENTS

I first visited Reading (by five different buses, from Titchfield, in Hampshire) in 1945, my great aunt having quit the ancestral home in the Isle of Wight and settled in the Palmer Park area. My first impression was of a pleasant town served by motor buses and trolleys dressed in a matt chocolate and dull cream coat. Totally unfair — practically everything had gone un-repainted during World War 2. On my next visit the fleet had re-emerged in claret-tinged maroon and well-stirred cream, with shine aplenty — a livery inherited from the trams and bejewelled with the attractive Reading coat of arms — very smart.

Only slightly 'out-county' — my first book was about Hants & Dorset — I began researching the history of transport in Reading in 1973, when records were held at Tilehurst Library, and soaked up a little historicity by lodging for a couple of nights at the George Hotel. Among those consulted in the 'Seventies were Mrs Winifred Binns, Vivienne Dabell, Miss M. A. Peebles ALA, Tom Pruett and Royston Jenkins, General Manager of Reading Corporation Transport — the latter a singular honour. It was about this time that I became aware of the research and published work of Edgar Jordan — to which he has added much since. Son of a local tramwayman, Edgar was the chubby-faced mascot of the Reading Tramways Football Team in 1920; if somewhat bigger, he is recognisably the same individual today. With the help of his large local archive Edgar recently related to me anecdotes and recollections about Reading's trams, trolleybuses and motorbuses — extra-spiced by his unmatched ability to put a name to each crewman's face. A delight to interview, he is a sound historian, highly articulate and witty. Should the local authority wish to honour a life-long citizen for services to the town's history, here is the man.

In late 2004 also, two senior officers of Reading Transport Ltd kindly made space in their very busy schedules and permitted me lengthy interviews. First, I am particularly grateful to Councillor Tony Page, a member of Reading's Transport Commmittee from 1974 and Chairman from 1986 — in which year he became Chairman also of the new 'arm's length' company, Reading Transport Ltd — for a refreshingly frank review. Secondly, Colin Thompson, Managing Director of the company, allotted some after-hours time to bring me up to date with recent history at the operations level. It is no secret that, in the 'Nineties, a series of potentially internecine events took place. Just how these difficulties were, in the main, surmounted by a continuing gentlemanly dialogue was related to me first by Colin Thompson and then, as part of a wider chronological history, by Michael Russell, currently Risk Manager of Reading Transport Ltd.

My thanks go also to Roger Davies, to Andrew Braddock, ex-Director of Operations for The Bee Line, to Derek Giles, ex-Traffic Superintendent of Southend Transport, and to Peter Davey of Bristol, for introductions; to Dolores Saunders of Reading Transport, for dealing patiently with my several requests for help; to Maureen Fowler and to Mel Atkinson, Manager of the Newbury Buses division of RT, for service updates, etc; and, for an historical perspective, to Sir George White Bt, of South Gloucestershire.

I received much help from the staff of the Berkshire County Record Office and of the Reading Central Library, in particular David Cliffe and Michael Hancock; similarly from David Shuttleworth and Stephen Berwick of the Harris Library, Preston and from Pauline Black of Birkenhead Central Library. Thanks also to Ian Ditchfield, for discovering there's next to nothing on the internet on Reading horse-drawn trams (until now), and to Jacquie and Andrew Waller.

Edgar Jordan, Alan Lambert, Andrew Waller, D. E. Wall and Michael Plunkett have made essential loans of material, the latter entrusting me with his lifetime's collection of Reading photographs, which just about made possible the whole project — a remarkable gesture, much appreciated.

And finally . . . a thank-you to the mellifluous Jo-Anne Sale, BBC Traffic Reporter and avid Reading FC supporter, who by some fluke always seems to be on duty in time to steer me around traffic problems whenever I'm travelling south. I'm pleased for her that Reading are high-flying.

Colin Morris
Heswall
August 2005

1. HORSE-POWER

Probably the first-ever 'transport logo' seen in the British Isles was upon a *c*50BC coin minted for Commius, King of the Atrebates. This Belgic tribe occupied the territory now known as Berkshire, northern Hampshire and Sussex. In the face of incursions across the Thames by the Catuvellauni — their hostile cousins — they retreated 10 miles to the south and founded the hill fort Calleva Atrebatum, thereby putting back the development of Reading by some 800 years. This brilliantly designed piece depicts what awaited Catuvellauni war-chariots, if . . . It also shows why stallions never horsed stage coaches, buses or trams. *Colin Morris (from a coin in the British Museum)*

Where to start? In the case of my previous municipal history, that of Bournemouth (2002), all was plain sailing — no-one lived there until 1810. Reading is somewhat older. Its geographical position suggests that Stone Age man was the first to use the locality as a base for three-way forays by dug-out canoe. But exactly when is anyone's guess.

So too is the matter of what 'Reading' actually means. Much conjecture has come forth over the years. 'It is so called from the British word — *rheden* — for the fern which formerly grew here in great quantity.' No, it's 'from the Saxon words *rhea* (river) or *rhyd* (ford) and *ing* (meadow)'. In the Vulgar Latin used by scribes in the early 13th century it was Rading on the Acqua de Kenete (Kennet Water); this became Reding (the way we pronounce it now), Redynges and, by the middle of the 16th century, Reddyng — and, 'of course', the name derives from settlement by 'Reada's people'. Take your pick!

Before the birth of Christ, agriculture, markets and means of distribution were brought to a sophisticated level by inter-related Belgic tribes. Living south of what was later called the Thames were the Atrebates. However, from across the wide river their cousins the Catuvellauni, under Cymbeline, began raiding the territory of the Atrebates. The latter promptly retreated to the south and built themselves a hill fort in the woods (at Silchester) — a move which put back the founding of Reading by some eight centuries. For, when the invading Romans chose the Atrebates as their allies, they showed them how to turn their fortress into a grid-pattern communications centre, surrounded by a still-surviving stone wall. This the Romans called Calleva Atrebatum. Of the five straight roads the Romans built from this, their main southern traffic centre, one set off north-westward for Corinium Dobunnorum (Cirencester). That built, the Romans rediscovered what that ancient Briton and would-be aviator Bladud had found ages before — the hot medicinal waters of Aquae Sulis (Bath, Somerset) — and built a special branch from the Cirencester road to reach it, setting off westward at a point just beyond Wickham (Berkshire).

Were it not for that ruffian Cymbeline then, the Roman road from Londinium to Bath may well have gone through what

became Reading — and who knows how much more quickly the town would have developed? I use the term 'town' advisedly, for, despite the signs, destination displays and tickets which today read 'City Centre', Reading (much to its civic disgust) has yet to be awarded this grand distinction. Cymbeline has much to answer for.

After the Romans went home Calleva fell into decline and the Atrebates and fellow Celtic tribes were driven ever westward — a process delayed by Vortigern, described by historians as a '*superbus tyrannus*' (a splendid name, perhaps, for today's branded route 17). The Danes, Alfred the Great and his Saxons, Henry I, Stephen and Henry VIII, for good or ill, all made their mark upon Reading, but none more so than Queen Elizabeth I, who looked kindly upon the town. She frequently resided here, and contributed by her munificence to raise the Corporation to the respectable state in which it has since appeared, hence the letters 'RE' (Regina Elizabet) which adorn the beautiful Reading coat of arms. I describe it as such for the younger generation, who may not have seen it, for it seems of late to have disappeared into the depths of the municipal offices, celebratory woolly rams and all.

By the 15th century the country goods-carrier with his 'long-wagon', travelling very long distances indeed — and quite prepared to take a few resilient passengers along with him — was established. Commuting into Reading, however, may be traced to those hitching rides on produce wagons attending the twice-weekly market. The carting of grain and wool formed a large part of such traffic before the 17th-century Civil War between the Royalists and Parliamentarians; long-distance travelling rather more comfortably by coach, originally only for the wealthy, had just got underway when vehicles and horses were commandeered by one side or the other, as both in turn laid siege to Reading.

Coaching was re-established, with improved vehicles, in time for the Restoration of the Monarchy in 1660. It was the resurgence of Bath, long in the doldrums, which sparked the elevation of Reading as a safe and comfortable haven astride a London–Bath road, which became renowned for the quality of its stage coaches. In 1667 'Flying Machines', so called because they could travel at 35 miles per day (as against the previous 20), left

4

The Belle Sauvage on Ludgate Hill, London, at 5am every Monday, Wednesday and Friday. The coaches were bound, after Reading and one other stop, for the White Lion Inn, Bath with six 'inside' passengers, each of whom paid £1 5s 0d (£1.25), and could carry 14lb in baggage free of charge, but were to pay 'three-half pence' for every pound in excess. The timetable was to be adhered to 'if God Permits' — and, presumably, highwaymen as well.

When Richard 'Beau' Nash was Master of Ceremonies in Bath (c1735) he had the Abbey bells in that city rung at the approach of each stage coach from London and Reading, for which the wealthy passengers delightedly paid the ringers, unaware that they were being assessed for their pedigree and social worth as they disembarked.

Specially built, or reconstructed, in Reading to deal with this traffic was a growing number of large inns: The George, with access in both King Street and Minster Street, The Ship Inn and Upper Ship Inn in Duke Street, The Broad-Face Inn (later The Elephant) in Market Place, The Angel in Butcher Row, Broad Street, and The Bull beside Cross Street in Broad Street. London Street to this day goes almost southward (rather than eastward) for some distance before turning eastward into London Road. Why? Because until the second decade of the 19th century there was no road to the east of a line High Street–King Street–Duke Street–London Street, the land being one of several areas around Reading liable to flood, hence the original coaching inns being gathered in the locations listed above. As coaching times were speeded up, the road from London to Bath was given a short-cut through Reading with the construction westward from London Road of New Street (soon

◄ Reading Market Place in full swing on an autumn Saturday morning, for bagged corn is up for auction. Morris dancers perform their fascinating routines before the obelisk, which, according to the inscription, was 'erected and lighted forever at the expense of Edward Simeon in 1804'. Because of the presence of so many parked farm wagons on the east side, coaches leaving the Broad-Face Inn (later The Elephant) were obliged on such mornings to depart via Friar Street and Abbey Street. Hitching a ride on one of these farm carts, however, was still a popular means of getting to town for shopping.
Colin Morris collection

◄ Down the B4000, a section of the original Roman road from Cirencester (Corinium) to Silchester (Calleva Atrebatum), comes Newbury Buses DAF SB220/Optare Delta No 506 (G506 XBL). Excavations along the route have revealed ruts left by Roman chariots (the original tramways?). On Tuesday 28 September 2004 the DAF leaves no such marks at Woodlands St Mary, running light from Lambourn to Newbury, ex service 4. Some four miles ahead, near Wickham, it will pass the spot where the Roman road from Silchester forked west to Bath (Aquae Sulis). *Colin Morris*

'The Telegraph' was a popular early-19th-century name for stage coaches in various places throughout the United Kingdom — so much so that the famous advance in suspension, the Telegraph spring, was named after one such, after it was fitted with the device. Reading's 'Telegraph' left Hone's coaching office in King Street for London at 12 noon, Monday to Saturday. Here it is passing Windsor Castle and Eton College Chapel one fine September afternoon in the 1820s. That sunlit cornfield is today buried beneath the M4. *Colin Morris collection*

List of stage coaches operating from Reading in the early part of the 19th century.

renamed Crown Street, after another coaching inn set up thereon), which joined up with a section of Southampton Street at that time called Horn Street; the coaches then went north up Seven Bridges Street, into Castle Street and onto the resumption of Bath Road.

The new relief road eased the accommodation problem, permitting other inns to be provided, but also led to the establishment of roadside booking offices — Keene & Co, S. & T. Williams and William Hone, all in King Street, Matcham & Loadsman at the Upper Ship Inn in Duke Street, The Sun Office and The Horse & Jockey in Castle Street, The Saracen's Head in High Street, The Peacock at 51 Broad Street (later a local omnibus depot) and the York House Coach Office at 129 London Street, the last primarily to deal with numerous coaches operated from a Bath hotel of that name.

Mrs Norris & Son of The Broad-Face Inn, Market Place, were active at the close of the 18th century, but the principal locally based stage-coach proprietors in the early 19th century were Jonathan Halcomb & Co, George Matcham and Samuel, Thomas & Samuel Jnr Williams, all of London Street, and William Hone, of 36 Castle Street. The last three had booking offices (see above) elsewhere in the town.

Two major technical advances in the first half of the 19th century struck first the local carriers and then the coach proprietors. First, in 1810, the Kennet Navigation was linked to the River Severn by the completion of the Kennet & Avon Canal. Reading, used to sea-coal from London, now had the more flammable Somerset-mined variety as well, to the benefit of fleeting visits from two famous pioneers — Sir Goldsworthy Gurney (1826), with his tiller-steered steam coach refuelled *en route* from London to Bath, and Walter Hancock (1835), on a trip to Marlborough in his 14-seat steam carriage *Erin*.

The second, permanent innovation — with far-reaching results for transport in Reading — was the coming of the railway. When, in July 1839, the Great Western line from

To London via Slough
Emerald
Gilder & Batten
Halcombe
Martin
Mattham & Co
Monarch
New Company
Old Company
Regent
Regulator
Royal Blue
Smith & Clinch
Telegraph
White Hart
Williams & Co
York House

To London via Staines

Accommodation
Comet
Forrest
Williams & Co

To Bath via Calne

Comet
Monarch
New Company
Old Company
Regulator
Star
York House

via Devizes

Emerald
Regent
Royal Blue
White Hart

To Southampton

Fowler & Co
Rocket
The Trial

To Oxford

Mrs Norris
The Dart
Oxonian

PLUS: The Dart to Cheltenham
Halcombe to Frome
Martin to Swindon
Industry to High Wycombe
The Oxonian to Portsmouth
Hero to Brighton

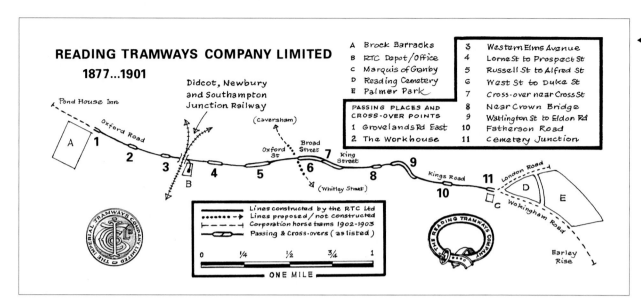

READING TRAMWAYS COMPANY LIMITED
1877...1901

Pond House Inn

Oxford Road

Didcot, Newbury and Southampton Junction Railway

(Caversham)

Oxford St

Broad Street

King Street

Kings Road

London Road

(Whitley Street)

Earley Rise

Wokingham Road

A	Brock Barracks	3	Western Elms Avenue
B	RTC Depot/Office	4	Lorne St to Prospect St
C	Marquis of Granby	5	Russell St to Alfred St
D	Reading Cemetery	6	West St to Duke St
E	Palmer Park	7	Cross-over near Cross St

PASSING PLACES AND CROSS-OVER POINTS

8	Near Crown Bridge
1 Grovelands Rd East	9 Watlington St to Eldon Rd
2 The Workhouse	10 Fatherson Road
	11 Cemetery Junction

- ●●●●● Lines constructed by the RTC Ltd
- ------→ Lines proposed / not constructed
- Corporation horse trams 1902-1903
- ◁▭▷ Passing & Cross-overs (as listed)

0   ¼   ½   ¾   1

▬ ONE MILE ▬

◄ The Reading Tramways Co Ltd, founded on 27 November 1877, with an ambitious nominal capital of £50,000 in 5,000 shares of £10 each, and a Registered Office at 3 King Street in the City of London, enjoyed an independent life of less than eight months. In July 1878 the Imperial Tramways Co Ltd purchased a controlling interest in both the Reading and Gloucester tramways companies from the Tramways & General Works Co Ltd of London, its contracting arm. RTC's operations were purchased by Reading Corporation in 1901, but the company was not formally declared 'wound up' until 1910.
Colin Morris collection

London reached Twyford, connections with Reading were made by displaced stage coaches acting as omnibuses. Thereafter, the stage-coach network from and through Reading was whittled away as the main line and each new branch was constructed. Thousands (rather than hundreds) per day could now be moved by the much faster train.

Coaches were now replaced by fledgling local omnibuses. The Peacock in Broad Street became the main exchange point for omnibus services not going to the railway station or the overcrowded Market Place. In the east there was, until the late 19th century, W. Embling's East End Omnibus Depot, whence this proprietor of the 'Reading & Earley Corn Stores' in London Road ran horse buses to the stations.

When, in August 1860, an American, George Francis Train, inaugurated his Birkenhead Street Railway he set in motion in Britain a mode of railed transport which was to remain in being for best part of a century. He employed as his earnest young tea-boy James Clifton Robinson, a native of Wirral, who was to become one of the most respected figures in British tramway history, earning himself a knighthood as a result. His name was destined to be trundled through the streets of Reading for nine years (1892-1901).

If William Forster's Education Act of 1870 succeeded in getting the 'up to 50 per cent of town children' who were 'running loose in the streets' into school, it was another piece of legislation in that same year, writ less large in the history books, which helped to get them there — or, rather, some whose parents could afford the ½d fare. This was the Tramways Act 1870, which stimulated the formation of several holding companies (such as the Provincial or 'Barber-Glenn' group in 1872), the aim of which was to construct and run urban tramways wherever they might be granted permission to do so. Such tramways already existed here and there, but the Act sought to regularise future schemes — generally to the advantage of the local authorities likely to be approached. Thus councils were given the right to veto such proposals completely or, in a clause which has been blamed for ensuring the poor upkeep of the independent tramways in their later years, the right to purchase the undertaking at any time after 10 years and before 21 years from the time of an Act confirming the relative local order.

In Reading's case the situation was, at the start, slightly different. An alliance between a construction company and a yet-to-be-formed tramways holding company was to rescue the initial plan for the town. First, the Reading Tramways Co Ltd was

founded on 27 November 1877, with its registered office at
3 King Street, in the City of London. Among its seven subscribers
were representatives of the Sheffield and Leicester tramways
companies, but, of particular note, two others were George
White, a stockbroker of Corn Street, Bristol, and Henry Hughes,
proprietor of the Falcon Works, Loughborough. None of the
seven, who subscribed £100 each, was a resident of Reading;
even the Secretary was based in London.

Secondly, an agreement was signed with the Tramways &
General Works Co Ltd to prospect, plan and construct the
proposed tramways in Reading. This firm, which did much of its
work by sub-contract, employed for the task its usual civil
engineer, Joseph Kincaid. The survey work and detailed plans
were complete by the end of the year. RTC's officers had noted
(like their successors in Reading) that the east–west route,
comprising tight-terraced housing with joined-up commerce at its
centre, would prove the most lucrative. George White, Secretary
— and effectively the managing director — of Bristol Tramways,
played a large part in the process. However, RTC's nominal
capital of £50,000 was to prove rather optimistic, and the sum of
£19,000 due to the T&GWC, in instalments, for its works, did not
look likely to be forthcoming, as the total amount of calls could
be counted in hundreds rather than thousands of pounds.

Accordingly, a holding company (of which a T&GWC director,
Alfred J. Lambert, would later gain control) was registered on 20
June 1878 as the Imperial Tramways Co Ltd, with four directors
under the initial chairmanship of Sir Rowland Blennerhassett,
Bart. Its registered office was initially at 4 Copthall Buildings in
the City of London, and its declared purpose was 'to purchase,
take upon lease, or otherwise acquire Tramway, Omnibus,
Railway, Telegraph, and Steamship Undertakings in the United
Kingdom of Great Britain & Ireland'. Sheffield Tramways was
involved in the formation of this company also.

On 17 July 1878 the Tramways & General Works Co Ltd
accepted from the Imperial Tramways Co Ltd shares amounting
to £166,750 'in respect of their interests' in the Dublin Southern
District Tramways Co, the Middlesbrough & Stockton Tramways
Co, the Corris Railway Co (in the counties of Cardigan and
Merioneth), the Gloucester Tramways Co (of which George White
was also a prime mover) and the Reading Tramways Co, the last
two being lumped together under the same indenture.

Thus the Reading Tramways Co became a subsidiary of the
Imperial Tramways Co, which would go on to acquire interests
in Bristol, Darlington, York and — in London — the West

Metropolitan, which became the famous London United
Tramways. At this point the original RTC directors were replaced
by those of ITC. George White, however, became a shareholder
in the holding company — and was destined to stage a powerful
comeback in 1892.

Meanwhile, as 1877 drew to a close, Reading Council formed a
Special Survey Committee to peruse the company's plans, drawn
up by Kincaid, which comprised a cross-section in detail of the
proposed work, showing the mode of construction. A line was to
be laid (in the T&GWC's preferred 4ft gauge) from the almost-
completed 41st Brigade Depot Barracks in Oxford Road to the
junction of Kings Road and London Road at Cemetery Junction
— some 2 miles 618 yards. On 9 March 1878 the company
announced that a proposed line through West Street, Caversham
Road and over the brick and iron version of Caversham Bridge
'would be abandoned for the present year, because of objections
raised by property-owners along that route'. Caversham residents
were not then rate-payers of Reading and, owing their allegiance
to Oxfordshire, called the proposed tramway 'a speculative
undertaking on the part of strangers to the neighbourhood'.
In the event, this offshoot was never built, more likely because
ITC discovered that Caversham Road was likely to flood —
as had occurred, disastrously so, as late as 1875.

The Kincaid system for the east–west 'main line' comprised
steel rails laid upon cast-iron chairs, 3ft from centre to centre,
each chair set in a concrete block 18in x 18in x 10in deep, the
depth from the rail surface (level with the road) to the bottom of
the concrete being 16in. The groove in the rail was about $1\frac{1}{4}$in.
The extreme width of the accompanying granite paving
demanded by Board of Trade regulations was 7ft $9\frac{1}{2}$in for a
single line and 15ft 7in when doubled. The whole of this surface
was to be made and maintained by the company.

Amendments and additions to the RTC scheme were made by
the Council. It adopted a clause which provided that, after a
dividend of 8% had been paid to shareholders, a moiety (one of
two parts) should be paid to the Corporation, which also became
a shareholder in the Reading Tramways Co.

The lengthy Order authorising 'the construction of Tramways'
was published on 6 April 1878. The 38 clauses included those
dealing with land, construction, improvements, penalties for poor
maintenance, plans, additional crossings, temporary tramways,
types of traction, types of traffic, carriage of goods, unfit carriages,
Sunday traffic (a hang-over from 17th-century Puritan legislation),
fares, luggage, workers' fares, carriage of animals and the

protection of the Corporation and the Gas Company, etc. The promoters were obliged to make all improvements in the tramway or rolling stock and were compelled to run two cheap-fare workmen's cars either way each day and to refrain from running on Sunday mornings. One year after the enabling Act they were to pay the Corporation a returnable with-interest security of £500.

The company was prohibited from purchasing or acquiring more than 5 acres within the Borough for the purpose of offices, stables, weigh-bridges, carriage houses, warehouses, works and 'connected conveniences'. In the event, it bought Norfolk Place, with an entrance between Nos 263/265 Oxford Road, with a frontage of 42ft. Later, in 1893, the area of the site was increased to 0 acres, 3 rood, 4 perches (3,652sq yd, or just over ¾ acre). It adjoined the east side of the Great Western Railway's 'Newbury, Hungerford & Southampton' branch line. Upon this site RTC built wooden-framed corrugated iron premises — stabling (on the east and south sides), a car-shed for eight single-deck trams, a smithy, a granary and a harness room. An office was provided in the house rented to local manager Mr O'Donahue at 1 Norfolk Place, whilst an auburn-whiskered and blue-uniformed inspector, Benjamin Hatt, was appointed and moved into rented accommodation at 301 Oxford Road.

Construction of the line was underway by October 1878, but heavy rains and a 4in fall of snow that December did not help. By February 1879 the work had 'progressed, but was not complete', and the Reading newspapers instead told stirring tales of the British invasion of Zululand and the fine example set by Lts Chard and Bromhead at Rorke's Drift.

Subsidence in Kings Road — and the fact that the Reading Gas Co chose to lay its gas mains at the same time — meant that only the western half of the line was ready by the proposed date. So, on Friday 4 April 1879, Board of Trade inspector Major-General C. S. Hutchinson was able to inspect and approve (with reservations) just the section between the Barracks and Broad Street. It was opened to the public the following day.

Imperial Tramways had decided that six 26-seater, four-wheel, seven-bay single-deck cars, drawn by just one horse apiece, would

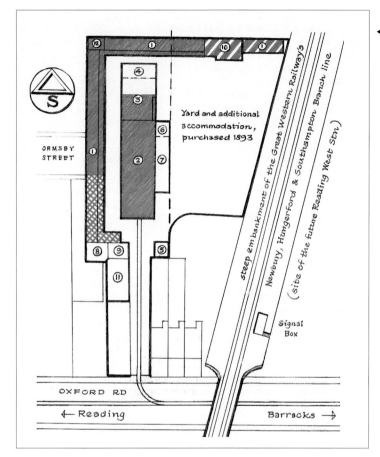

The Reading Tramways Co Ltd established its depot on a plot in Oxford Road. At its greatest extent (1893-1903) it comprised: stabling (1), tram shed (2), blacksmith's (3), carpenters' shop (4), sawdust store (5), lamp room (6), mess room (7), harness room (8), stores (9), granary (10) and manager's house and office (11). The toned area represents that consumed by fire in 1893, the striped area neighbouring property purchased subsequently; the hatched area is the firebreak created by troops from the Barracks.
Colin Morris collection

suffice for the Reading system. There is sufficient evidence — photographic and documentary — to conclude that the trams were of a standard type built in Stephenson/Starbuck style by Henry Hughes, an original RTC subscriber. Although it will take sophisticated electronic tests to prove it, their original colour scheme was most probably red and cream. Initially there were just 30 horses at the depot, but arrangements were made for four to be housed in stables behind the Marquis of Granby Hotel, when the eastern section was opened for public service, on 31 May 1879. Quickly proven to be inadequate in number, the six

The initial Reading Tramways Co fleet of 1879 comprised six 24- or 26-seat, seven-bay single-deck cars, each drawn by one horse. The latter is attached to a curved tow-bar known as a whippletree, in turn secured at the appropriate end by a removable cotter-pin dropped into the frame. The horse, either a mare or a gelding, looks in peak condition (if a little long-legged for the task), although it has probably brought the car straight from the depot to Grovelands Road East, near the Barracks, but a short distance away. The car, No 4, is in the original RTC livery, ivory and — probably — red; no-one seems to know for sure. *Edgar Jordan collection*

trams were nevertheless described as 'commodious and handsome'; in them, stated a surprised *Reading Observer*, 'high and low, rich and poor deigned to sit shoulder to shoulder'. Soon, however, there were reports of irregularity of service, times not being kept, passengers being left behind, overcrowding and smoking in carriages. In addition the points were open (not adjustable), the horse having to be pulled onto the correct line. Frequently a driver failed to do so, causing two sets of horse and tram to face each other on the same track. Not much had changed by September 1879, for an astute correspondent with the *Reading Observer* noted that boy conductors (some of whom wore blue caps lettered 'RTC') made sport of passengers, giving oblique answers to questions about departure times — 'If you're goin', you'd better get in' — delivered with an impudent stare. They used language 'unfit for ladies to hear' when helping the driver bring around the horse at the termini and, rather more loudly, to their colleagues when they passed another tram going in the opposite direction. Drivers, who did not wear any kind of uniform, seldom received 'a bell' from the conductors and started off when they thought fit. He encountered over-crowding to the point of suffocation and found that in Oxford Road passengers wishing to go east got on cars going west, so that cars arriving at the Barracks were already too crowded to board. 'Viator', as he called himself, called cogently for comfort, convenience and civility and — doubtless having seen such things in London — 'some kind of number, or means of identification'. The Council, good but not noted for speed, duly issued licences and badges with numbers — in 1885!

Meanwhile, back in 1879, mounting evidence of poor management may have cost Mr O'Donahue his job, for by 7 October he had been replaced as RTC manager by a Mr Stokes. On that date ITC's answer to the problems of suffocation, passengers who smoked and the use of bad language whilst changing the horse from one end to the other manifested itself with the delivery of car No 7, built and patented by Henry Hughes' Locomotive & Tramway Engineering Works. A 28-seater, it was divided into two compartments — non-smokers being accommodated in the enclosed and comfortable front half, smokers in an open-sided rear. In addition the body revolved upon the framework of the truck; the horses remained attached at the termini, being brought around simply with 'hard right' rein. Hughes (of Loughborough) built six for use in Britain, including one for ITC's Gloucester Tramways. At least one more ran in Paris for Les Tramways Sud — or so I believe — for Hughes was supplying tramway equipment to that company in 1879; it ran through the 12th, 13th and 14th *arrondissements* between Place de la Nation and Porte d'Orléans (see illustration). The British examples were probably panelled to the waistrail, contrasting with the Gallic solution, which featured a low fender-grille to arrest discarded cigarette packets; even in the days before Gitanes and Gauloises the French smoked particularly pungent tobacco.

Car No 7 in the RTC fleet was a rare vehicle 'patented' by its builder, Henry Hughes of Loughborough. Non-smokers sat in the front half, 'puffers' at the rear. At the termini the body was swung around on its chassis. Six are known to have worked in Britain; this one, run by Les Tramways Sud de Paris, was probably built to Hughes design also (see text) and is shown to illustrate the principle. Around she goes: the conductor undid the cotters, disengaged the brake cable and carried the end in a smaller arc than the side-stepping horses. In Reading they would have been pulled to the right. *Colin Morris collection*

With the delivery of car No 7 the directors of the Imperial Tramways Co Ltd — now minus George White — considered Reading adequately provided for. The only change of note was the replacement in 1883 of Mr Stokes by the 'courteous' Frederic Groves, who set about pleading with ITC for improvements. The ITC board, based, from 22 May 1888, at 57½ (sic) Old Broad Street, London EC (within strolling distance of the Stock Exchange and the Bank of England), now comprised Alfred J. Lambert (Chairman), Colonel Edward Gourley and William Ward, with John W. Alison as Secretary. This team, regarding Reading Tramways as the most profitable in their portfolio, let the concern drift, so long as it paid a dividend. For the best part of a decade after Groves' arrival the old problems persisted — unless No 7 came along.

In London, however, all was not well — the shareholders had become dissatisfied with the performance nationally of ITC. At the General Meeting of August 1892 all the serving directors were asked to retire from the board. Back into the fold, as Chairman, came George White. James Clifton Robinson,

ex-General Manager of Bristol Tramways, and a highly respected tramwayman internationally, became Managing Director. Hugh C. Godfrey, solicitor to the North Metropolitan Tramways, among others, joined the board, and Samuel White was appointed Secretary. The headquarters of Imperial Tramways was promptly removed to Clare Street House, Bristol. Fred Groves' difficulties at Reading were about to be eased considerably.

Probably the first noticeable alteration was a change in livery for the trams. Photographic evidence suggests a version of the early-style Bristol Tramways livery — a bilberry (dark) blue and cream. The new board laid plans to upgrade the standard and upkeep of horses in the group and to listen more sympathetically to the advice of local managers like Groves. It was, however, a dramatic event at 3.50pm on Thursday 11 May 1893 which gave an unexpected kick-start to significant improvements at Reading.

An alert soldier at Brock Barracks reported a large pall of smoke rising from a point just beyond the railway bridge — the tramways depot was on fire. A large stack of straw had been

Photographed after the ITC headquarters had transferred to Bristol, this tram appears in considerably better condition than the horse. The poor creature looks underfed, dispirited and worn out. Car No 3, at the terminus in Oxford Road, is painted in the early Bristol Tramways-style livery and lining-out pattern. Beneath the stock (fleet) number is an 'end-on winged wheel', apparently the Imperial Tramways badge. Above the windows, dropped into a bracket, is the letter A; letters A to F indicated the running order of each car. The roof ventilator is closed on what was probably a chilly day.
Michael Plunkett collection

ignited by a spark from a nearby forge. The officer of the day assembled 50 troops, some armed, together with a crew equipped with the 3rd Royal Berkshire Regiment's horse-drawn steam fire engine. They got there first, to find that the stable lads had at least freed the horses, some of which had galloped off east and west. While some of the troops cleared the narrow entrance of unhelpful onlookers, Major Edwards assessed the developing scenario — the tram shed and a large section of stabling being well ablaze — and ordered the demolition of an unburned section of the latter as a firebreak to save nearby housing. Smart thinking? Well, apparently not, for at this point the Malden Erlegh (*sic*) Brigade, with two engines, and the Reading Volunteer Fire Brigade from Chain Street turned up with 10 men and a hose-cart under the command of the Head Constable of Reading. The latter, dressed in civvies, began a stand-up row with Major Edwards claiming, it would seem, that (a) the troops shouldn't be there and (b) the unburned stabling should not have been torn down. The Head Constable in turn was told he was an insubordinate, impertinent nincompoop — or something similar.

Whilst this comedy of errors was being staged, all the stabling, a 30ft granary and the 90ft tram shed were destroyed, the latter with five tramcars, only their ironwork remaining. Also gutted were the neighbouring brick stables and coach house belonging to Deverell's Oxford Lodge next door.

After the company's stud had been rounded up and found lodgings at various stables made available locally, a paper war was fought between military and civil authorities. Asked Colonel Borrett, OC 49th Regimental District: 'Should we then not render assistance in the event of fires in the vicinity?' To which Mayor Martin replied, in that eccentric style of judgement not entirely dead in high places, to the effect that yes, they'd like the military to turn out in the event of fire 'for the special purpose of keeping order in the streets', but that 'Major Edwards, before commencing

to knock down stables, should have sought the directions of the Head Constable before doing so'. Yet, as everyone knew, he wasn't there at the time! One sensible outcome of this absurd spat was that it led directly to the establishment of the full-time Reading Borough Fire Brigade.

Samuel White, writing from Bristol to the *Reading Observer*, anounced that Fred Groves had 'made arrangements for running the usual service of cars', and asked that 'any unavoidable inconvenience' be overlooked. That five cars had been destroyed at that time of day implies that at least nine single-deck cars had been made available for Reading by the Bristol headquarters before the fire. Whether it now sent more or whether Groves hired local horse buses to maintain the service is not known, but this may be when plans were laid to introduce eight new horse buses to the fleet (a number confirmed by the Head Constable's report in 1896).

George White and his fellow directors moved quickly not just to restore but to improve the equipment of RTC by providing new tramcars, horses and harness at a cost of £2,000. On Saturday 15 July 1893 six new 33-seater double-deck cars ('garden'-seated on top and probably built by G. F. Milnes & Co of Birkenhead) were launched into service with considerable ceremony. For the first time two horses were attached to each car, which on the opening weekend presented a very lively appearance, with flags flying from their tops and with drivers and horses wearing rosettes.

On the day the new cars entered service the ITC directors visited Reading to inspect the system and decide upon a site for a new depot. Joseph Greenaway, architect, of 19 Duke Street was asked to draw up plans for a new depot and works at Grovelands Road East (on the east side of Brock Barracks), estimated to cost £3,000 to erect. He did so, but instead it was decided to rebuild and enlarge upon the original site, adding land and buildings previously part of Oxford Lodge — but still, in the main, with wood and corrugated iron.

The 700,000 passengers per annum carried by the old single-deck cars were expected to rise to 1 million with double-deckers in use. This new fleet was increased piecemeal by an additional five second-hand double-deck two-horse cars, most likely ex-Bristol Tramways; Nos 7-9 and 11 were fitted with 'knifeboard' seating on the upper deck, whereas No 10 looks as though it may have been 'garden'-seated. Surprisingly, a photograph exists of all 11 RTC double-deck trams and Nos 1 and 8, at least, of the company's horse buses.

From June 1896 RTC's horse buses competed in turn with four others purchased from the London General Omnibus Co Ltd by Edwin Allan Harrison of Brigham Road, Reading, to run in competitive extension of the tram route, from the Pond House Inn to Earley Rise. Harrison traded as The Favorite Express Bus Service — a name always 'corrected' to 'Favourite' in the Watch Committee records (and repeated as such thereafter). But 'Favorite' was one of the LGOC's several regional fleetnames, this one acquired with James Wilson's fleet of that name in 1856; a decade earlier Wilson had adopted and part-anglicised the identity of the Paris-based Les Favorites. The LGOC kept the name 'Favorite' on many of its horse buses until they were withdrawn in 1911. Harrison's pictured 'knifeboard' Favorite, which was probably still in its original livery of red with yellow wheels, seems to have retained its London depot-plate bracket on the front offside corner-post.

The Reading Tramways horse buses tagged along behind the 'intruders' at a flat fare of 1d, but RTC reduced its tram fares: Barracks–Post Office, Post Office–Cemetery and Trinity Church–Factory Bridge journeys cost 1d; beyond those distances the fare was 2d. Harrison then dropped his 'all the way fare' to 1d, and competition became very keen. As a result of the low fares all

Just how the tramways manager, Fred Groves, kept the tramways running at anything like an adequate frequency in the aftermath of the destruction of the RTC depot by fire is not made clear in the local papers of 1893. It may well have been this which triggered the purchase of eight horse buses for RTC (the Head Constable's report for 1896 confirming the number) from Alex Dodson's works in London. No 1 is pictured at the Earley Rise (Wokingham Road) terminus. Despite the livery they may have remained the property of ITC, for they did not pass to RCT. *Edgar Jordan collection*

Following the disastrous depot fire in May 1893 the directors of the parent Imperial Tramways were obliged to send replacement trams to Reading. Somewhat belatedly they made the grand gesture and provided for the town its first double-deck tramcars, new and up-to-date. On Saturday 15 July 1893 car No 2 — facing west toward the Barracks — has emerged from the depot, the latter's entrance just visible above the head of the lad on the costermonger's cart. Like its five companions, No 2 is starting its first day's work. *Walton Adams / Michael Plunkett collection*

At the other end of the line — Cemetery Junction — car No 2 has been joined by No 3. The latter's horses have been detached and are being exchanged for a pair from the RTC stables behind the Marquis of Granby Hotel (right). The whippletrees (towing brackets) have yet to be brought around to the westward-facing end, ready for the return journey. Local schoolchildren in their weekend best form the majority of the spectators; beyond, visible between the two trams, is an onlooker astride a parked Starley 'Royal Salvo' tricycle, built *c*1881. *Walton Adams / Michael Plunkett collection*

Cars 1 and 6 meet at the Victoria Square/Fatherson Road stop in King's Road. Again, well-dressed local folk have turned out to watch the intermittent inaugural parade, the horses wearing rosettes beneath their ears, and the trams bedecked with temporary poles bearing flags fluttering the company's colours. The broad-footed numeral '1' on the eastbound car, the lining-out and the 'closed-scissors' decorative device at its corners are pure George F. Milnes & Co, as adopted by Bristol Tramways; James Clifton Robinson's name is on the rocker panel beneath. *Walton Adams / Michael Plunkett collection*

15

In this amazing period-piece photograph, car No 2 has come to a halt at Jackson's Corner, beside High Street, whilst No 5 tackles the rise up King Street. On the right is J. & C. Simonds Bank; beyond, in Broad Street, are George Palmer's statue, Wellsteed's Stores — whose advertisements featured large upon the rocker-panels of several horse trams — and the Boar's Head inn. Here, in the centre of town, the numerous onlookers are setting the precedent for subsequent crowds who turn out to watch each 'first' or 'last' transport event in Reading. *Walton Adams / Michael Plunkett collection*

READING TRAMWAYS COMPANY.

NOTICE.

ON and after Saturday, July 15th, an accelerated and improved Service of Cars will run in accordance with the following

TIME TABLE.

SUMMER — 1893 — SERVICE.

WEEK-DAYS.

UP.

Barracks ..	dep.—	8. 0 a.m. and every 10 minutes till 10. 0 p.m.
Trinity Church	,,	8.10 a.m. and every 10 minutes till 10.10 p.m.
Post Office.	,,	8.15 a.m. and every 10 minutes till 10.15 p.m.
Factory Bridge	,,	8.25 a.m. and every 10 minutes till 10.25 p.m.
Cemetery ..	arr.—	8.30 a.m. and every 10 minutes till 10.30 p.m.

DOWN.

Cemetery ..	dep.—	8.30 a.m. and every 10 minutes till 10.30 p.m.
Factory Bridge	,,	8.35 a.m. and every 10 minutes till 10.35 p.m.
Post Office..	,,	8.45 a.m. and every 10 minutes till 10.45 a.m.
Trinity Church	,,	8.50 a.m. and every 10 minutes till 10.50 p.m.
Barracks ..	arr.—	9. 0 a.m. and every 10 minutes till 11. 0 p.m.

SUNDAYS.

Cars run every 10 minutes, the first leaving the Depôt for Cemetery at 1.40 p.m., the Barracks at 2.0 p.m., and the last Car will leave the Barracks at 9.30 p.m. First Car will leave the Cemetery at 2.0 p.m. and the last Car at 10.0 p.m.

FARES.

Barracks and Trinity Church		
Trinity Church and Factory Bridge	}	1D.
Factory Bridge and Cemetery		
Beyond above distances or all the way		2D.

The Company will not be responsible for the punctual running of the Cars, but will endeavour to maintain regularity.

FRED GROVES, Manager.

Traffic Offices, Oxford Road,
Reading, July 13th, 1893.

What can only have been Reading Tramways Co's 'knifeboard' car No 9 — its rails being of a different shape from No 8's — is trotted west along Broad Street. The conductor has a good excuse for sitting down for a chat with the top-deck passengers rather than attending to the one about to board the tram, for the vehicle is clearly on the move. The picture was taken somewhere between No 9's acquisition in 1895 and its enforced retirement in late 1898, when it was one of two cars found to be too wide to comply with the rules of the Board of Trade. It certainly looks bulbous. *Michael Plunkett collection*

This 'knifeboard'-seated (upon the upper deck) two-horse tram has all the characteristics of one which has been built or refurbished in the workshops of Bristol Tramways. It lacks the Starbuck-style arched tops to the windows, but the top-deck drain vents (beneath the advert on the decency board), the shape of the dash, the staircase stringer, the stair rails and the forward-sloping canopy are strong pointers to its origin. With just a few passengers inside, No 11 heads west past Duke Street, the horses walking calmly, unperturbed by a small terrier on the loose. *Edgar Jordan collection*

An ex-London General 'Favorite' (see text) of Edwin Allen Harrison's 'Favorite Express Omnibus Co' (launched in May 1896) at Earley Rise, the eastern terminus of his route from the Pond House, Oxford Road. Although mis-matched, the horses are an extremely fine pair, the conformation of the grey, particularly, looking ideal for the job. In contrast, the horses of the attendant Reading Tramways omnibuses are at least two hands shorter and look exhausted by their efforts to give chase. Even their driver seems to be doing an agitated jig — but has the consolation of two schoolboys aboard for the white-knuckle ride. *Michael Plunkett collection*

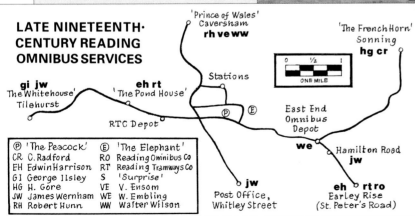

LATE NINETEENTH-CENTURY READING OMNIBUS SERVICES

'Prince of Wales' Caversham
rh ve ww

'The French Horn' Sonning
hg cr

Stations

gi jw
The Whitehouse' Tilehurst

eh rt
'The Pond House'

RTC Depot

East End Omnibus Depot

we

Hamilton Road
jw

jw
Post Office, Whitley Street

eh rt ro
Earley Rise (St. Peter's Road)

0   ½   1
ONE MILE

℗ 'The Peacock'	Ⓔ 'The Elephant'
CR C. Radford	RO Reading Omnibus Co
EH Edwin Harrison	RT Reading Tramways Co
GI George Ilsley	S 'Surprise'
HG H. Gore	VE V. Ensom
JW James Wernham	WE W. Embling
RH Robert Hunn	WW Walter Wilson

Basing their operations upon two town-centre inns, the Peacock in Broad Street (landlord James Wernham) and the Elephant in Market Place, a dozen or so individuals ran temporary bus services, until the Corporation extended the tramlines. The odd-man-out was Walter Wilson, whose service was run by motor buses.
Colin Morris

vehicles were well patronised. The trams ran a more frequent service — which helped wear out the elderly track. One horse bus collided with a tram, and the rest competed furiously at a loss — until Harrison gave up. The tram fares were immediately increased, and the RTC horse buses sent elsewhere by ITC, probably to avoid compulsory purchase by the Corporation. Pounding hooves and frantic tram-driving left the permanent way an easy target for municipal criticism. The Corporation had been the real beneficiary of this near free-for-all.

In 1898 Reading Corporation began to apply pressure upon RTC. On 10 November it was resolved 'that the Head Constable do take all requisite steps for enforcing the Byelaws and Regulations . . . relative to tramways and to the drivers and conductors of tramcars'. Samuel White had already written from Bristol in August 1897 — 'You will remember that [in] the case of Nottingham [which corporation had just acquired the Nottingham & District Tramways Co], where the council had anticipated the purchase period by a year or so, [it] had paid the par value of the shares'. On that basis, the ITC/RTC directors would come to Reading for discussions.

The Town Clerk, Henry Day, replied that 'any basis which would be less advantageous to the Corporation than the terms prescribed [in] the Tramways Act 1870' would not be negotiated upon. The ITC/RTC directors did not come to Reading.

Meanwhile, in the autumn of 1900, motor wagonettes of around 10hp each, which had been pottering around town frightening the horses several years before, were first licensed for excursion work. Much of the latter was in connection with Edward Cawston's 'Trips on the Thames' premises at the centre of the iron version of Caversham Bridge, where passengers went down a series of steps to join his steam launch *Eclipse*, an elegant 60-seater. The 10hp MMC 'Granville' 12-seater wagonette was considered ideal for the task.

Whether or not with his own vehicle is not clear, but extending his knowledge of wagonette operations from November 1900 was Arthur Julian, of Julian & Sons, cycle agents, of 37 Market Place.

The Watch Committee granted him Council driver's licence No 150 and conductor's licence No 27.

Julian's contribution to British motor-omnibus history has gone largely unsung. Because of the laying of new tram lines which followed in Reading, he turned his attention to Portsmouth. There he founded Portsmouth & Gosport Motors Ltd, inaugurated on 4 January 1902, when it carried a party which included the mayor and council officers of Portsmouth. The vehicle used was a 16-seater, the 'Cambria' comprising a lorry chassis by G. F. Milnes & Co Ltd, with a German Daimler engine; more importantly, it was the first Milnes chassis fitted with a bus body, again by Milnes, and as such was the prototype for the famous Milnes-Daimler company, founded in November 1902, whose vehicles gave a proper start to motor-bus services throughout the United Kingdom. Furthermore, a deputation from Birmingham went south to see for themselves and returned home to found the Birmingham Motor Express Co, which in 1904 became the pioneer of motorised passenger transport in that city. This has previously been described as a feather in Portsmouth's cap, but the credit should really go to this citizen of Reading.

The first licensed stage-carriage motor buses in Reading were the MMC wagonettes of the Reading & District Motor Car Co, set up by Walter Wilson in May 1901. Three of the four-strong R&D fleet of 10hp 12-seaters are lined up in the appropriate dawn's early light; their hand-built individuality is obvious. The conductors included Fred Whale, William Clements and Fred Coombes, the drivers Alfred Harms, Henry Pennell, John Jackman, Fernand Barthelemy and Charles Brooker, although one drove the single MMC run by Pugh & Strode of Castle Crescent.
Colin Morris

Of the 13 omnibuses licensed by the Watch Committee to operate stage-carriage services within the borough in 1896, just one was the property of A. G. Watson. He ran his operation from an office in King Street and clearly had expansionist intent, for the vehicle was labelled 'The Reading Omnibus Company'. His lone two-horse omnibus is seen passing the Vine Hotel into West Street, *en route* to Caversham. The Council put paid to that a couple of years later, as it cleared the way for the laying of its own tram lines along Caversham Road. Too little, too late!
Michael Plunkett collection

Yet Julian returned to Reading, to take an active part in the setting-up of Jordan's garage, dealing in motor cars.

A near neighbour of Julian's, at 27/28 Market Place, was Walter Wilson*, estate agent and Secretary of the Reading

& District Mutual Plate Glass Insurance Co. He was possibly in partnership with Julian when, in May 1901, Wilson founded his appropriately named Reading & District Motor Car Co Ltd, which ran stage-carriage services between Market Place, Friar Street, Stations and Caversham, pausing on the bridge for the boat traffic. The fleet comprised three MMC 'Granvilles' and a 'Balmoral'; in bad weather these were fitted with glass-windowed canopies, so that they could serve year-round in all weathers.

One other MMC was approved for Messrs Pugh and Strode of Castle Crescent; they had asked for three licences but were granted just the one. By early 1903 all five MMCs had fallen foul of the Corporation's tram-line works, and both motor and horse-drawn buses disappeared from the Reading scene — the latter forever.

* This was not the engineer of the same name credited later with the concept and original design for the world's first military tank in World War 1 and with innovations in motor-bus design.

The fourth MMC — a 'Granville' — in the Reading & District fleet was this one, which operated between Market Square and Caversham. It is parked, facing south, on the iron version of Caversham Bridge, beside Edward Cawston's mid-river 'Waterman's Cottage' booking office, in the summer of 1901. Whilst awaiting further passengers from a river cruise the driver adjusts the timing on the 10hp Panhard-Daimler engine. He is possibly Arthur Julian, a neighbour of the proprietor and a pioneer whose influence was to extend far beyond the confines of his native Reading (see text). *Colin Morris*

2. CORPORATION TRAMWAYS

Although car No 4 of 1893 vintage does not appear to have had its image recorded on its debut in Reading, it seems to have succeeded on 31 October 1901. On that day Reading Corporation — after protracted negotiations — took over all the assets of the Reading Tramways Co Ltd. Despite its somewhat worse-for-wear bolt-on enamelled advertisements it was probably the smartest one left in the depot when it was sent to pose in Broad Street with a complement of similarly transferred employees, to mark the occasion. Depot men and boys occupy the top deck, the driver wears a newly issued uniform, and Inspector Benjamin Hatt (see text) still has his job. *Walton Adams / Michael Plunkett collection*

The formal and regularised involvement of the Borough of Reading in the provision of its own public passenger transport could be said to have commenced with the setting-up, on 10 October 1898, of its Tramways Committee. Its brief was to 'transact and have charge of all business conducted with existing and future tramways in this Borough', including the purchase of the Reading Tramways Co's operation.

The 14 members of Council attending the first meeting included the Mayor, Alderman Berkeley Monck (chairman) and Alfred H. Bull, one of the most prominent tradesmen of the town, soon to become mayor himself. The members' first resolution was to instruct the Borough Engineer, John Bowen, to examine the lines and works of RTC, thus setting in motion the process by which the latter could be prevailed upon to part with its undertaking at minimum expense to the ratepayers of Reading.

With the exception of short stretches which had been re-laid with girder rails, Bowen found 'the whole of the permanent way in a very defective condition' and that it was 'a daily occurrence for the cars to fail to take the points if a new . . . driver happens to be in charge . . . or when new horses are hauling'. The points were found to be in need of repair at the termini, the cross-over near Cross Street and all eight other passing-places along the line.

Bowen's astute argument was that the company should not be compelled to carry out extensive rail renewals, as (i) it would then be entitled to payment according to structural value, and (ii) such new rails would not be suitable for mechanical traction anyway. Instead, he was of the opinion that the line should be, in effect, 'jacked up a bit' where necessary and have all the points renewed. Of the 10 cars in operation, he found two which were simply too wide to permit the Board of Trade-required 15 inches between trams when passing each other. Since Nos 1-6 of 1893 were built to a common pattern, these must have been two of the second-hand additions. They were promptly withdrawn from service. He also noted worn wheels on some of the remainder, reminding Groves that 30in chilled-cast-iron wheels cost only £3 14s per set, In fact G. F. Milnes charged £7 per set.

For its part, ITC tried unsuccessfully to entice a deputation of councillors to Bristol to look at the electric tramway system running there since 1895, as a result of James Clifton Robinson's enthusiasm for this mode of traction. The Imperial Tramways Co had, after all, achieved the distinction, in July 1893, of obtaining from Parliament the first tramway Act specifically empowering it to construct an electric tramway system — that of its Dublin Southern District Tramways subsidiary. Noting this at the time, the local newspapers had expressed the hope that it would do something similar for Reading; ITC certainly had the expertise to do so. However, the Corporation now had the bit between its teeth and was determined that (a) there would be an electric tramway system in Reading and (b) it would be owned by the Council.

Planning began in detail. The 4ft gauge would be retained; 'when the new [Queen Victoria] street is formed, a tramway should be laid from Reading Station to Broad Street' (though laid it never was), an electricity-generating station provided, and 'an electrical engineer and expert' engaged to advise the Council and the Borough Engineer & Surveyor on how to start the whole business.

Most surprising, considering the sheer scale of work involved, was the choice of the old St Giles Mill in Mill Lane as the site for a completely new electric tramway depot. It was necessary to demolish the mill and its huge water tower (but keep the bricks), cover over (or campsheath) the Mill Tail stream at its junction with the River Kennet, build a dam across Gunter's Brook (to allow for the filling-in of the Mill Head), enlarge Tan Lock to a width of 40ft and overcome objections from the Great Western Railway, which had earlier acquired proprietorship of the Kennet Navigation in order to hold that competitor at bay; the GWR was now concerned that this relatively dormant part of its property would 'be injured'. Parliamentary powers and the approval of the Railway Department of the Board of Trade had to be obtained for each step, the latter particularly in order to effect the acquisition of the Reading Tramways Co.

For the latter, the Council offered the company's directors £10,105 — which was promptly rejected. A panel of inspectors was sent to assess the assets of RTC. Capt J. A. Ford (Horse Superintendent, London County Council Tramways) inspected the stud, Norman Scott-Russell of the Brush Electrical Engineering Co Ltd the rolling stock, and George Woolley

(Manager of Works, LCC Tramways) the harness and stores, a separate team of four examining the permanent way. Sir Frederick Bramwell, the referee appointed by the Board of Trade, assessed the value of RTC as £11,394 — and that's what Reading Corporation paid for it in October 1901.

The only real setback at this time was that the Urban District of Caversham again flexed its independent muscle and rejected Reading's terms for a line of tramway extending into Caversham's territory — and trams were destined never to cross the Thames.

Meanwhile, Frederic Groves agreed to act as manager of the now 'Reading Corporation Tramways' for a period of two years at a salary of £350 per annum: and the services of the existing tramways employees were retained at their respective existing wages. Their expertise was indispensable, as the Council now found itself responsible for two vastly different systems of operation — setting up the magical infrastructure of electric traction but in the interim continuing to serve the travelling public with the existing but complex world of horse-drawn tramways. The unusually large membership of the appointed Tramways Committee was entirely justified.

Various sub-committees found themselves asking the Council to pay for: horses from Tomkin's Horse & Carriage Repository in Friar Street (at a time when a bay gelding cost £35), harness oil, disinfectant powder, horse clippers, new harness, feeding baskets, gaiters and clogs, sawdust (from Huntley & Palmer's — what *were* those biscuits made of?), grey winter oats, English black Tartar oats, Russian oats, maize, straw, sainfoin (or 'Holy-Hay' — a type of vetch), mangolds, halter ropes, cod-liver oil, sacks, condiments, horse nails and shoes, files, outside grazing for recuperating horses, the services of Wheatley & Son (veterinary surgeons), new whippletrees, new uniform caps, badges and overcoats, the cost of printing tickets and the royalty on Bell Punch machines, forage and stall bedding (from nine different suppliers) and a host of other incidentals, on a scale far larger than the familiar needs of their own household pony and trap.

Two additional inspectors were appointed, both conductors and drivers were supplied with overcoats and caps, drivers' wages were increased by 6d (2½p) per day, the horses had their daily forage ration increased from RTC's 16lb of corn plus hay to RCT's 20lb, and stablemen were granted a holiday once in every nine days. A tip (or third) horse was outstationed and ridden by a 'tip-horse boy' each day, to Factory Bridge to help tram horses up the (then) 1-in-16 inclines, and the stud was raised to its maximum of 72.

The Corporation found that eight of the 10 cars it had inherited were fit for further service and so decided to purchase three second-hand trams, to bring the interim fleet up to 11, in order that a 7½min frequency could be timetabled. The cars, surplus to the needs of Portsmouth Corporation Tramways (more advanced in its electrification scheme than was Reading), were brought up via Winchester and Newbury by the GWR (at a cost of £8 3s 11d) and carried from the station to the depot in Oxford Road by LSWR steam wagons (£5). Total cost of the three, plus carriage, was £60 11s 11d. F. E. S. Theake was paid £8 18s 0d to clean and paint each car in the newly chosen municipal livery of maroon (claret) and cream, but the more drastic alteration necessary was to the gauge, Reading's being 7¾in narrower than Portsmouth's. Three replacement sets of Milnes axles, wheels, springs and journal boxes were purchased (cost not given), and the resultant holes in the lower panelling covered with a strip of beading.

The three, which had constituted Portsmouth's '60' class (its smartest), represented the acme of horse-tram construction, having been built for Provincial Tramways by William Harding & Co Ltd of Lune Street, Preston, in 1894 (The associates of Dick, Kerr & Co Ltd did not arrive in that town until 1897). Harding's trams were described by the *Lancashire Daily Post* as having a 'beautifully decorated interior . . . a thing of beauty and a joy forever'. Well, not quite; these three were licensed in January 1902, for just 18 months' further service in Reading. The name of Henry Day, Town Clerk, appeared on the rocker panels and now replaced that of James Clifton Robinson on those cars purchased from RTC.

To launch the new era, three basic contracts were awarded:

1. The construction of new tramways, the electrical bonding of the rails and the provision and laying of conduits for the underground work, with drawing-in boxes — Edmund Nuttall of Manchester (with Bolckow, Vaughan & Co of Middlesbrough as manufacturers of the rails)

2. The provision of (a) boilers, stoves and superheaters, (b) economiser, (c) piping, feed pumps, hot well, tank etc, (d) engines, (e) condensers, air pumps, circulating pumps etc, (f) electric generators, (g) switchboards and connections, (h) lighting of buildings, (i) overhead, (j) hand-powered travelling crane, (k) motor trucks, (l) electric motors, controllers, car wiring and erection, (m) car bodies and (n) trolleys — Dick, Kerr & Co Ltd, Preston (there having been a total of 81 tenders for this contract)

3. Plans, sections and specifications for the buildings and for the generating station — Arthur Hill of Sparrow Hill, Loughborough

Much of this work and the manufacture of the necessary equipment was sub-contracted to other firms. For instance, the

On the very day that it took control of the horse tramways, Reading's Tramways Committee took stock of its eight roadworthy cars and decided that it needed two or three second-hand ones as a stop-gap. In December 1901 the Corporation took delivery of three William Harding cars from Portsmouth Corporation's horse-car fleet, the latter in course of replacement for the same radical reason. Although in fact third-hand, they were handsome vehicles. Seen *circa* June 1903, a mis-matched pair of horses wait beneath the new electrical overhead at Cemetery Junction as a very large passenger climbs aboard. *Michael Plunkett collection*

Lorain Steel Co in the United States received such accurate drawings for the four-way, double-tracked West Street junction that, when the parts were laid out in Reading, they fitted perfectly. The building of the 10-road tramcar sheds, the generating station and its 150ft chimney became the task of R. W. Blackwell & Co Ltd. In relation to today's (2005) Reading Transport, it is worth noting that Nuttall located his works depot and materials-assembly point in Great Knollys Street (named after the Knollys family, several members of which had represented the Borough in Parliament until 1760).

Seven-inch-deep heavy steel rails replaced the horse-tram tracks on the 'main line', which was extended west to the Pond House Inn and east to Earley (Wokingham Road), a branch being added from Cemetery Junction to 'Sutton's' railway bridge in London Road. A north–south route was built from the southern approach of Caversham Bridge to Whitley Street, whilst a short branch westward was taken up Castle Hill, into Bath Road. The basic network was completed by a line which went beyond the Mill Lane Depot turn in Duke Street and followed the original 18th-century stage-coach route along London Street and the western end of London Road (as far as Craven Road),

A member of the Tramways Committee from its inception, Alfred H. Bull — he who owned more department stores in the town than several others put together — was elected to a third term as Mayor, in time for the grand opening of the Corporation's electric tramway system. Thus, on Wednesday 22 July 1903, it was Alderman Bull who set the great day in motion. After the dignitaries, in 10 of the new cars, had enjoyed a free round-trip, the trams were made available to the public (who paid). No 6, still displaying 'Erleigh Road' but going the wrong way, has encountered a temporary spot of bother beside the Vine Hotel. *Walton Adams / Michael Plunkett collection*

Ladies in elegant Edwardian dresses move to board a pristine car No 23 at the Pond House Inn terminus in Oxford Road. This one is bound for London Road, along the 'main line' via Broad Street. Its trolley-boom is still attached to the distant wire — a common occurrence at this stage, even if the tram used the southern track beside Craig Avenue. All was sorted out as the car re-joined the single track as far as the Barracks, but what happened if a second tram arrived at the terminus? Like its sisters, No 23 is fitted with side destination boards — not as delivered, but affixed soon afterwards. *Michael Plunkett collection*

Like some beautifully marked insect emerging from its chrysalis, one of the half-dozen five-bay Dick, Kerr 70-seaters slides out into the light between the huge doors of the main car shed. It is a bogie-car, self-articulating four-wheel trucks carrying its extreme length safely around the curves. This one is already marked up for Oxford Road. Indeed, these cars, delivered in 1904, were intended primarily for use on the 'main line' — a long-vehicled theme destined to be repeated upon that route. The power-station chimney looms in the mist. *Michael Plunkett collection*

terminating at the eastern end of Erleigh Road. It was along this last stretch that the first tram motormen were taught to drive by instructors from Dick, Kerr & Co Ltd, as part of that firm's tender and contract.

The total capital cost of setting up the electric tramways was in excess of £223,000. Not an engineer, Fred Groves became Traffic Superintendent for RTC when, in April 1903, Walter Binns, Senior Engineer of Newcastle upon Tyne Corporation Tramways' power station, was appointed Engineer to Reading Corporation, at a salary of £300 per annum. Presumably the Council kept quiet about what Groves was being paid.

The initial fleet of electric trams comprised 30 double-deck four-wheeled cars which, like all passenger-carrying trams that ran in Reading, were open-topped — the scant clearance under Oxford Road and Caversham Road railway bridges saw to that. The trucks (chassis) were of the Brill 21E type, fitted with two Dick, Kerr 25hp DK25A motors, driving wheels of that same 30in diameter as those on the horse trams. The 50-seat bodies were built by the Electric Railway & Tramway Carriage Works Ltd of Preston (associated with Dick, Kerr & Co Ltd through the presence of John Kerr on both boards of directors from 1897), to that firm's standard three-bay design employed nationwide — in Reading's case with reversed stairs. The trolley equipment was provided by Dick, Kerr also.

Ornate overhead traction poles stand at intervals down the length of Oxford Street — the eastern end of Oxford Road, under which name the 'street' was eventually subsumed. Tram No 4 is held at the Cork Street stop to take on board a 'last-minute' father and very small son. The car is travelling westward on the 'main line' to the terminus at the Pond House. To the right is the impressive façade of McIlroy's department stores, known locally as 'Reading's Crystal Palace' — a remarkably bold piece of architecture for the time, matched only by the wonder of tramcars which moved without horses. *Colin Morris collection*

Gliding smoothly eastward down Broad Street comes car No 18 *en route* to Wokingham Road. It is high summer, and the top deck is filled with lightly clad passengers — both men and women wearing that smart Edwardian unisex item, the straw boater. The tram has just passed the grand entrance to the Market Way Arcade, wherein was to be found a tramway lost-property office — after, that is, the local police had reluctantly given up responsibility for such things. Car 18 is also about to pass the statue of George Palmer, of biscuit fame. *Colin Morris collection*

The conductor and driver of car No 20 pose for the camera on the platform at the eastern terminus of the 'main line' route from The Pond House to Wokingham Road. The former has yet to change the destination blind to read 'Oxford Road'. No 20 is at the original terminus of the line, the cross-over being opposite Brighton Road. Going westward as far as Crescent Road, Earley Rise, the line was double-tracked, but from there to Cemetery Junction was a single track with two passing-loops. Just a few years earlier, competing horse-buses paused beside these trees. *Michael Plunkett collection*

A fine specimen of the ornamented centre-poles erected ▲ at several points on the electrified system; this one, in King Street, opposite what is now Barclays Bank, displays a red disc, warning tramcar drivers that this was the location of a section insulator, at which they were required momentarily to shut off power. Another centre-pole stands in the entrance to Duke Street — the way home for the trams. Beyond it the overhead is carried on pairs of bracket-armed poles. Outside the bank, six members of the Reading Ebony Minstrels raise some extra cash. *Colin Morris collection*

Up the lower section of Castle Street comes Dick, Kerr three-bay car No 13, travelling west on the first of three double-tracked sections of the Bath Road route; in earlier times stage coaches between London and Bath trundled up this same hill. The tramcar is passing St Mary's chapel (1799), an offshoot of St Giles. The writer of the card, postmarked 26 August 1905, attended Sunday-evening services there because 'the Caversham trams pass the door'. At the extreme right is Edward Morris's Corn Stores, supplier earlier of fodder for the Corporation's tram horses. *Michael Plunkett collection*

▲ Despite travelling the length of Broad Street, these are not acting as 'main line' trams. No 9, coasting down into King Street, is on its way to Erleigh Road, whilst No 4 is on a journey to the 'corrected' destination, 'Caversham Rd', both being 'side routes'. The addition of advertisements has changed the cars' appearance considerably — for the better, perhaps. *Michael Plunkett collection*

Rebuilt to this quarter-turn-staircase format in the 'Twenties, Dick, Kerr tram No 24, built like its companions in 1903 as a 48-seater, gained two extra seats in the process. A coloured light route indicator, previously set in the reverse staircase stringer, is now in an ornate box, useful also for the driver's 'bits and pieces'. The light for this destination, Erleigh Road, was violet. Ironically, the car is pictured at the same spot where sits (in 2005) what appears to be a miniature tram bound for Bristol; a closer look reveals a hot-dog stall!
Colin Morris collection

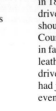

Although a thoroughly informed contributor to the *Reading Observer* in 1879 — a gentleman calling himself 'Viator' — urged that the drivers and conductors of Reading's passenger-carrying vehicles should wear 'some number or means of identification', it took the Council some little while to get around to organizing it — until 1885, in fact. This was the result — a 3½in enamelled metal plate (on a leather thong) which quickly distorted the wearer's jacket. 'Tramway driver No 65' was issued in 1910 to Herbert Edwin 'Tim' Jordan, who had joined RCT in 1906, became a conductor in 1908 and would eventually rise to the rank of inspector. *Edgar Jordan*

For use almost exclusively on the 'main line', six additional trams were delivered in 1904. These were very large 70-seat bogie cars, ideal for moving rush-hour traffic east–west, mounted on Brill 22E trucks with Dick, Kerr DK6A motors of 35hp each. Bodywork was again by ERTCW, the whole being supplied by Dick, Kerr. On these 33ft 6in cars the stairs were of a half-turn normal layout, which meant that the motorman had a clear view to his left. The first was introduced to passenger service in Reading on 29 July 1904.

The first financial year of operation with all 36 trams available saw 8,018,428 passengers carried, for a profit of £2,923 — a large part of which came from the display of advertisements around the upper panelling. From January 1910 route destinations were additionally identified by one of six differently coloured lenses in a rotatable housing, carried initially in both staircase stringers — blue (Bath Road), orange (Caversham), violet (Erleigh Road), green (London Road), white (Whitley) or red (the 'main line', in both directions). It took until 1929 to overcome the difficulty experienced by other road users at night, as to whether a stationary 'red' car was 'coming or going'. A blue and white quartered lens (like a BMW badge) was substituted and (as Edgar Jordan points out) from a distance of 30ft or more looked white — the same as the Whitley route.

Walter Binns, sporting a well-groomed military-style moustache of the kind much admired by the ladies in the early 20th century, ran the department with an iron discipline, difficult to countenance even in those days. The slightest perceived misdemeanour could result in a repeated daily dressing-down for up to a week — a terrier-like persistence. Yet in 1912 he improved the working conditions of drivers and conductors, reducing their weekly hours from 65 to 60 and granting them one day's rest in seven. With the tramways in good order he departed that October for an appointment overseas, to be succeeded as General Manager by his assistant, George F. Craven.

In 1911 the Urban District of Caversham — north of the Thames — was transferred from Oxfordshire into an expanded Borough of Reading; this, together with a 1913 attempt by the London & South Western Railway to gain powers to run motor buses from its railway stations, added impetus to a Council review of its future transport needs, begun in February 1912. Much midnight oil was burned deciding whether to extend the tramways or establish a service of rail-less trolleys or motor omnibuses in connection with the tramway. The resultant Reading Corporation Act 1914 left all three options open.

As far as the tramways were concerned, the main theme was to get the tracks across the Thames into Church Road, Caversham, over what it was hoped would be a reconstructed Caversham Bridge, approved in the Reading Corporation Act 1913. The outbreak of World War 1 (1914-18) put back that reconstruction by more than a decade, and dreams of a tram line over the Thames were placed upon what turned out to be a permanent back-burner. Also put to bed, for the duration of the war and beyond, was Craven's agreement with union requests for glazed vestibules to be fitted to the trams as weather protection for motormen.

By early 1915 some 35% of the operating staff had left to join the armed forces. At the end of that year the first women were taken on as conductors — under the care of a woman inspector — and worked a 48-hour week. Two years later 75% of the male staff had been called up, and some women had been trained to drive the trams. By the end of the 1916/17 financial year, however, well over 10 million passengers had been carried on the trams, and in 1918/19 the figure rose to nearly 16 million. By the summer of 1919 many of the men had been demobilised, and women crew members had departed from the platforms of the trams.

In January 1920 George Craven accepted an appointment elsewhere, later (until 1947) serving as General Manager at Halifax Corporation Transport (and writing a commendatory foreword to Edgar Jordan's first book in 1956). Upon his departure he recommended that, in turn, his assistant James M. 'Jimmy' Calder — a likeable Scot with a good sense of humour — should become his replacement. The Council agreed, and to Calder would fall the tasks of seeing the tramcars through to the end of their days, planning and supervising their replacement by trolleybuses and laying the foundations for today's motor buses.

Car No 21, rebuilt but never given vestibules, passes beneath the old brick-built Great Western Railway bridge at Reading West, just before its replacement in 1938. A new horizontal-span girder bridge meant that the 25-year-old 'Keep your seats' signs could be dispensed with also. A Board of Trade inspector had insisted they be put there (and on Caversham Road railway bridge also) in 1903, following a detailed safety inspection on site.
The otherwise double-track along Oxford Road became single beneath the brick version, to bring each car in line with the crown of the arch. *Edgar Jordan*

The nationwide General Strike of May 1926 affected the running of trams in Reading, as it did in most municipalities, because the Corporation allowed its workforce to participate in the trade-union movement. The territorial bus companies at that time tended not to, but Reading eschewed help from that quarter. Instead, it ran a flat-fare skeleton service, with the manager and a few members of staff from Mill Street as drivers; an 'honesty box' and a policeman riding shotgun on the step completed the *ensemble*. Stage 2 rebuild No 17 heads west at West Street Junction. *Michael Plunkett collection*

Like all save one of the four-wheeled cars, No 23 was rebuilt by RCT in the 'Twenties to this quarter-turn, direct-stair layout and from three-bay to a stronger four-bay format. Probably to keep the vertical canopy-supports rigid, a horizontal bar was incorporated in the structure. For a shortish motorman this impeded his line of vision — and appeared to be a potential hazard for all of them. *E. Byrne / Colin Morris collection*

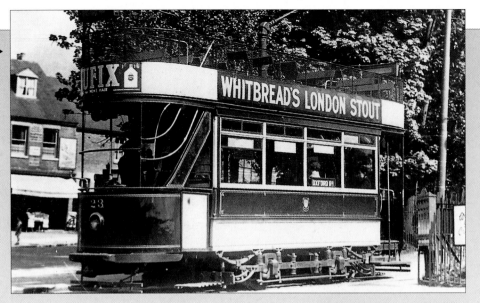

A good weekly source of income for the tramways — even the reserve matches attracted a goodly crowd in those days — was the home games of Reading Football Club. On Saturday 19 February 1927 Broad Street has been closed to all other traffic as a good-natured and orderly crowd is shepherded into the street to over-fill the trams for Kensington Road — the nearest stop to Elm Park, Reading FC's ground. Later that day the 'Biscuit Men' beat Brentford 1-0 in the FA Cup, before a crowd of 33,042 — more than have ever gone to a football match in Southampton. The car in the middle is No 19. *Edgar Jordan Collection*

Motorman Chaplin looks relaxed aboard No 8 at the Oxford Road terminus during the latter days of the trams, when they had plain-cream rocker panels. The car is one of 13 fitted with vestibules from 1925 onwards, more than a decade after Calder had planned to provide them. Difficult to please, some drivers complained that they found them 'draughty'. *W. A. Camwell*

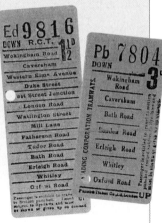

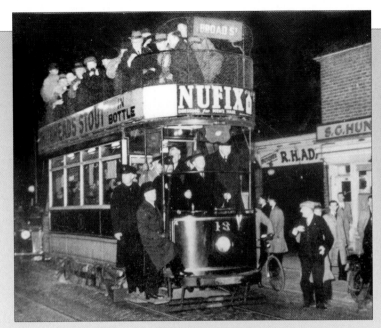

Reading's official 'last tram' — appropriately No 13 — departed from the Oxford Road terminus for the depot on Saturday 20 May 1939. James Calder rides on the step as motorman William Drew lets Councillor Palmer have a go at the controls. On the earlier 'last car' from London Road (No 21) Edgar Jordan's father 'Tim' was the motorman; it can't do any harm now to disclose that the young Edgar 'had a go' at driving that one! *Berkshire Chronicle*

Built by Dick, Kerr on a Brill 21E truck and purchased in 1904, No 37 was an electric-powered rail-grinder, whose main task was carried out nocturnally. It was known by the staff as 'the water-cart', its most obvious feature being the large water-tank carried amidships. A multi-purpose vehicle, it was also fitted with large snowploughs, which rescued several cars in the depths of winter. It is pictured in 1937, its fleet stock number probably chalked on by the photographer, an avid tramway enthusiast. *W. A. Camwell / Colin Morris collection*

Conductor Stone poses at the London Road terminus with 'two Tims' — motorman 'Tim' Jordan (father of the photographer) and a TIM ticket machine, which type was used at one time or another on all three types of passenger-carrying vehicle in the Reading fleet. The tram, vestibuled car No 9, is marked up for a short journey to Wantage Road in the summer of 1938. *Edgar Jordan*

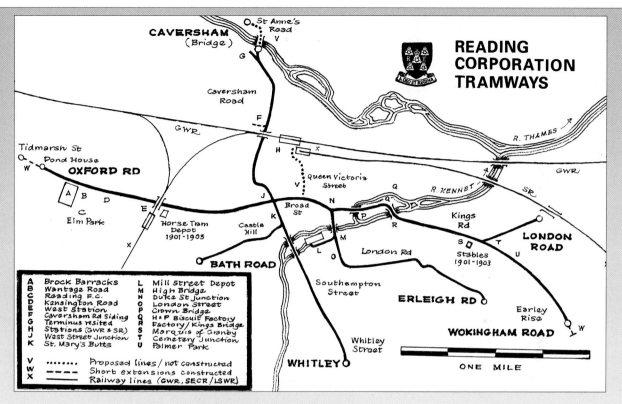

READING CORPORATION TRAMWAYS

A	Brock Barracks	L	Mill Street Depot
B	Wantage Road	M	High Bridge
C	Reading F.C.	N	Duke St Junction
D	Kensington Road	O	London Street
E	West Station	P	Crown Bridge
F	Caversham Rd Siding	Q	H & P Biscuit Factory
G	Terminus resited	R	Factory/Kings Bridge
H	Stations (GWR & SR)	S	Marquis of Granby
J	West Street Junction	T	Cemetery Junction
K	St. Mary's Butts	U	Palmer Park

.... Proposed lines / not constructed
- - - - Short extensions constructed
——— Railway lines (GWR, SECR/LSWR)

ONE MILE

The map of the system, depicted here, does not differentiate between sections of double or single track; it was largely of the former. In contrast to most other UK systems, there were few extensions to that originally laid. Like the earlier versions of the word 'Reading', 'Earley', 'Erleigh', 'Early' and Erlegh are all etymologically correct and appear at various points in the history of the tramway. *Colin Morris*

3. TROLLEYBUSES

Credit for the invention of the first embryonic trolleybus is given by transport historians to Werner von Siemens, who on 29 April 1882 unveiled and demonstrated his 'Electromote' — a five-seat wagonette — at Halensee, Berlin. Thereafter much of the development of the 'trackless trolley' took place in Austria and Germany, the first such public service running in 1901. Spurred on, perhaps, by George Craven's professional awareness of trackless trolleys in Yorkshire a decade later, the Tramways sub-committee set up in Reading in 1912 sent a deputation that September to inspect a Cedes-Stoll 24-seat demonstrator running for one week along Greengate Street, West Ham, its overhead strung between West Ham Corporation's tram wires.

So it was that when the Reading Corporation Act 1914 empowered the Council to improve its passenger-transport system, it included permission to pursue the establishment of a trackless-trolley service in support of the tramways. Mooted were five sections, principally a nominal 'service 3' between Caversham Bridge and Harrogate Road, Caversham Heights, and another between the Railway Stations and Prospect Park; when the proposed new and wider ferro-concrete version of Caversham Bridge was constructed, it was planned to connect these two sections to create a through service between Caversham Heights and Prospect Park. It was estimated that the provision of trolley vehicles and overhead would cost £6,800 and would require a 10-year loan.

Then, of course, came World War 1, and projects large and small were put on hold. Quite apart from that, equipment and parts necessary to keep in being those primitive systems already set up in the United Kingdom were now behind enemy lines. It was not a propitious moment to pursue the matter in Reading, and at the end of the war there was no early prospect of the new bridge being built.

In March 1919 the Tramways Committee was told that no useful object would be served by too close a consideration of the trackless-trolley project. The Council was aware that the portion between Caversham Bridge and Harrogate Road could have been undertaken but decided that a detached section requiring separate electrification was not desirable. It also noted that the original estimated cost had now spiralled. What money the Council could then afford was instead spent upon refurbishing the tramways and launching a fledgling motor-bus service.

The long-planned ferro-concrete bridge across the Thames was at last opened to traffic in 1926, but in that decade trolleybuses for Reading had become a dormant issue. Eventually, towards the end of 1931, a Tramways (Future Policy) sub-committee was charged with considering how and when the tramways system should be replaced. Deputations headed by James Calder visited several authorities already operating trolleybuses. The majority view in Council was that trolleybuses should be run solely on the Caversham Bridge–Whitley Street route, but, at the suggestion of the Parliamentary agents, when the Reading Corporation Act was promulgated Reading had obtained powers to substitute trolleybuses upon all of the remaining tram routes.

Where, 32 years earlier, electric tramway motormen had been trained to drive — on the Erleigh Road section to the eastern end of Addington Road — trolleybus wires were erected, for a similar purpose, in March 1936. The selected personnel honed the necessary skills on this Sunbeam MF2A/Park Royal 50-seater — a second-hand works demonstrator built in 1933. *Michael Plunkett collection*

Early in 1936 a Sunbeam demonstrator trolleybus visited Reading and was tried out at dead of night on the Whitley Road tram route, trailing a sparkling skate in the tramline to complete the electrical circuit; Edgar Jordan thinks this may have been what became Reading trolleybus No 1 (RD 8085), which arrived fitted with a skate. The vehicle was towed — by converted AEC YC bus No 1 (DP 2362) — back and forth between Mill Lane depot and Erleigh Road, where Calder had set up a length of trolleybus overhead, on tramway standards, for driver training. He discovered that, on average, a bus driver got the hang of the new skills in 50 hours, but a tram driver took nigh on 100. Whatever, it was along the length of Erleigh Road that Reading's first trolleybus drivers honed their early skills.

Calder, ever painstaking and cautious, elected to try out several makes of trolleybus on the Caversham Bridge–Whitley Road route (C), seeking to write a specification embodying the best points and noting such things as energy consumption; defects on contactors, traction motors, commutators, power wiring and lighting; brakes (electrical and mechanical); air-compressor units; resistances; transmission parts and batteries. The vehicles proved for the trials were numbered 1 (RD 8085), Sunbeam MF2A/BTH (ex-demonstrator), 2 (RD 8086), AEC 661T/EE, 3 (RD 8087), Guy BT/EE, 4 (RD 8088), Leyland TB4/GEC, 5 (RD 8089), Ransomes, Sims & Jefferies/EE (nicknamed 'the Lawnmower' — RSJ made those also) and 6 (RD 8090), Sunbeam MF2A/BTH (a new one). All had bodywork by Park Royal and, because of the restricted headroom under Caversham Road railway bridge, were of lowbridge configuration.

Whilst motor buses covered the route for two days, Clough Smith & Co Ltd, using materials manufactured by the British Insulated Cable Co, converted the overhead from tram to trolleybus specification. With due ceremony, five of the trial vehicles were launched into full passenger service on the morning of Saturday 18 July 1936. As a portent of its career to come, the RSJ was missing that day.

Some 15 months later a decision had been reached: the winner was the AEC. Meanwhile, explained James Calder in 1939, '. . . we possessed some very well-built brick buildings which were erected to house trams. From a bus or trolleybus point of view they were useless'. These were demolished and replaced by a depot measuring 180ft by 187ft, to provide cover for 60 vehicles 'without a single obstruction in the form of a pillar or post', completed just before the outbreak of World War 2 on 3 September 1939.

A provisional Order in 1936 had permitted that motor-bus routes which were actually extensions of existing tram routes should be converted to trolleybus operation. Thus the Wokingham Road terminus was earmarked for extension to the Three Tuns at Earley, and the Oxford Road/Tidmarsh Street terminus to The Plough, Tilehurst (and on to the Bear Inn), with a turning-circle at the junction with Norcot Road. This extended the 'main line' considerably, to six miles in length, against the 1½ miles of the north–south route. Meanwhile, the Mill Lane main sub-station was converted from tram to trolleybus supply, with capacity raised from 400kW to 1,000kW. Four additional sub-stations were built along the main route, with capacity ranging from 150kW to 300kW, all five together supplying power to all four points of the routes compass.

By 1939 Jimmy Calder, President of the Municipal Passenger Transport Association, was a leading champion of the trolleybus, at a time when the majority of its members were protagonists of the diesel-engined motor bus. Ironically, George F. Craven, his erstwhile boss and mentor, was making his name nationally with supercharged-diesel experiments at Halifax, but the two men remained very good friends.

▲ The five follow-up competing trolleybuses, purchased new, seated 52 passengers apiece — and were somewhat heavier than the second-hand No 1. Tyres bobbling over the setts and tram lines at West Street Junction No 2 (RD 8086), comes an AEC 661T model with English Electric equipment. Correctly marked 'Whitley Street', it was, like the others, fitted from the outset with two blue lights beneath the upper-deck front windows, presumably to show it was a trolleybus; motor buses sported white lights.
The Omnibus Society

Recognisable at a glance by virtue of its high-mounted headlamps, which, in effect, pushed the sidelights up above the maroon dash, No 3 (RD 8087) was the representative for Guy Motors Ltd of Wolverhampton. The firm must have had high hopes for success, because its Guy BT/EE model incorporated several novel features. Most noteworthy was that the forward location of the motor permitted a lower floor height. Although the propeller shaft was much longer, the working angle of the universal joints was considerably reduced. *Ian Allan Library*

Leyland's competing contribution to the lengthy trial period was No 4 (RD 8088), a TB4 model with General Electric Co equipment, the only Reading trolleybus so fitted. Maybe this helped bring about its being — marginally — the heaviest (at 7ton 11cwt 3qr) of the triallists. As with its five rivals, its Park Royal bodywork was of lowbridge configuration to permit clearance beneath the GWR's bridge over the Caversham Road. This official Leyland photograph shows it at the Caversham Bridge turning-circle on the opening day. *Michael Plunkett collection*

Towards the end of World War 2 the fifth of the initial sextet of trolleybuses performed its most notorious act. By then No 105 (RD 8089), the Ransomes, Sims & Jefferies/ English Electric/ Park Royal, had been collected from the depot by a driver who had just stepped out of the cab of a motor bus; upon turning into Bridge Street he attempted to use the power-pedal as a clutch. The unfortunate vehicle knocked the railings of the Gunter's Brook–Mill Tail Kennet Navigation into the water — not, as reported elsewhere, into the Holy Brook, nor did the bus follow the debris.
Michael Plunkett collection

No 6 (RD 8090) was Sunbeam's up-to-date contribution to the trials, being the 54th MF2A model off the production line. It was the lightest of those built in 1936 for Reading Transport's 'competition route' (C) between Whitley Street and Caversham Bridge. At £2,067 it was only £3 more expensive than the cheapest of the five, the ill-fated Ransomes, Sims & Jefferies. The Sunbeam Trolleybus Co Ltd, also of Wolverhampton, was destined later to become a subsidiary of Guy Motors — and, eventually, of Jaguar Cars Ltd.
Ian Allan Library

The Associated Equipment Co Ltd was deemed to be the winner of the trolleybus trials, and 25 AEC 661T models, with English Electric equipment and 56-seat highbridge bodywork by Park Royal, were purchased to replace the trams on the 'main line' with effect from 21 May 1939. From the outset those working eastward displayed 'Three Tuns', which gave the idea for a World War 2 'alternative destination' identity scheme designed to confuse the enemy. In this 1939 photograph, however, No 111's companion, No 129, shows 'Horncastle', which should have fooled everyone, for no trolleybus ever went there. *The Omnibus Society / Michael Plunkett collection*

Purchased to service the tramway's electrical overhead, this Leyland Badger tower wagon, bodied by Eagle Engineering, spent most of its 27-year career doing similar work in support of Reading's trolleybuses. Photographed prior to delivery, on 4 March 1937 at the Leyland works in Lancashire, RD 8892 bears the fleet number TW3, in sequence with the horse-drawn example (miraculously surviving with the praiseworthy British Trolleybus Society) and its immediate predecessor, based upon a retired AEC YC bus chassis. Later renumbered 32, it would be joined by a Commer tower wagon (No 33) in 1946. *Michael Plunkett collection*

No 126 (ARD 689), in a slightly travel-worn condition, is pictured at the Tilehurst terminus in 1951, together with two fellow AEC 661T trolleybuses. Their highbridge bodywork had proved suitable for the 'main line' route since the restrictive brick-arch railway bridge in Oxford Road had been replaced in 1938, with a metal horizontal-span version. Nevertheless, the twin-trolley poles dipped to near-parallel with the buses' roofs as they passed beneath it. The trees seen behind the vehicles would later succumb to development, being replaced by a line of shops. *C. Carter / D. E. Wall collection*

During the summer of 1938 the Great Western Railway replaced the original brick railway arch in Oxford Road (with its clearance of 16ft 3in), building in its place a plate-girder structure of constant height. Thus the 25 AEC 661T/Park Royal 56-seater trolleybuses — Nos 107-31 (ARD 670-94) — were of highbridge configuration. The first five of the batch were put to good preliminary use in advanced driver training and Ministry of Transport driving-test work on the newly constructed Tilehurst section. From Sunday 21 May 1939 the AECs replaced the trams on the new 'main line' trolleybus route.

Upon the outbreak of World War 2 Reading was declared a 'safe area' suitable for the reception of evacuees. The population rose accordingly, and the municipal buses were worked to the limit. As men were once again called to the colours, women were recruited to conduct the vehicles. This time they remained, and to this day ladies are well represented upon the driving staff. The continuance of electric traction meant that Reading was able to make a modest contribution to wartime fuel economy.

Whether it was a so-called Baedeker raid or a lone Dornier on a free-range mission is not known, but a bomb dropped

Perhaps regretting its decision to dispense with trams just before the outbreak of World War 2 and suffering, like all other operators, from shortages of liquid fuel, RCT was relieved, in 1943, to be allotted six utility trolleybuses. These were Sunbeam W/English Electric/Park Royal 56-seaters — and no-frills in every respect. No 134 (BRD 799), on a short run to Norcot Junction, was the only one to receive a postwar upgrade, including a rebuilt front, a large destination screen over the platform — and its little blue lights. All six were withdrawn in 1950. *W. J. Haynes*

behind Wellsteed's stores at the corner of Broad Street and Minster Street broke a window in AEC trolleybus No 119 (ARD 682) as it was passing at the front. This was a separate incident from the notorious 'People's Pantry' raid on the Market Arcade. Was Reading a legitimate target for attack? Well, it is doubtful if the Luftwaffe knew that Spitfire components were being manufactured at (among others) Vincent's and Caversham Motors garages, for they remained in operation. Meanwhile, in order that any German parachutists might not identify their location, the stone plaque in Mill Lane proclaiming 'Reading Corporation Tramways Power Station' was boarded over — an act which was to save it for posterity.

Unfortunately for James Calder, the war postponed the planned extension of the trolleybus system on the scale which he had devised. He was, however, able to lay hands upon six new utility trolleybuses, delivered in time to supplement an extension of the 'main line' westward to the Kentwood roundabout. The technical and financial components inherent within a transport manager's job are complex at the best of times; in Calder's case, the former required a high degree of concentration and skill as he wrestled with wartime difficulties coming so quickly upon the detailed work associated with the change from trams to trolleybuses. Anyone doubting the degree of specialised knowledge necessary should delve at any point into the 719-page, 27-chapter 'basic' handbook *Electric Traction*

by A. T. Dover (published by Pitman in 1929); you'll soon give up! Small wonder that a pair of little lights, borrowed from the trams, appeared over his office door — a red signifying 'Don't disturb me — I've almost got it right', a green 'Yes, please do come in'. Yet Calder was considered by his staff to be reasonable and popular, a fact perhaps best illustrated by his immediate concern at discovering a young employee working way beyond hours, mending TIM ticket machines: 'Good Lord, do go home, and give my apologies to your mother for keeping you out so late!'

Briefly a temporary inspector during World War 1, Edgar Jordan's father Herbert Edwin Jordan was again appointed to that rank in 1940 and in Calder's latter days became one of the two senior inspectors known as Traffic Regulators, keeping things moving in Broad Street or putting in a fatherly appearance anywhere else on the system, should a crisis develop.

Upon James Calder's retirement in 1945, his deputy, J. F. Fardell, must have expected, according to custom at Reading, to be appointed in his stead. However, the Council for the first time chose otherwise, selecting William M. Little from St Helens Corporation Transport. The comparatively youthful Little soon proved to be simply 'in transit in his career' and moved on the following year. Another previously rejected candidate applied again and was this time successful. He was William John Evans from Cardiff Corporation Transport Department, where, as Engineer, he had been locked into an unsatisfactory 'joint-headship' with a Traffic Manager. At Reading he became the last 'Transport Manager & Engineer' of the department. During his period in charge the trolleybuses were to enjoy their glory days in the town, until, as elsewhere, the infrastructure of such systems fell victim to major road-realignment schemes and difficulties with spares as other operators consequently transferred their affections to the motor bus. Ironically, it was to the continuing benefit of the latter that Evans was to make his major contribution to municipal transport in Reading.

The six Brush-bodied Karrier E6 trolleybuses which actually served in the RCT fleet, Nos 158-63, were kept going with spares quarried from the other half-dozen, given the 'chalked-on' numbers 164-9. Suitably refurbished, the first of the active examples (No 158) took to the road in late 1948, the last (161) in 1951. These veterans served on both the east–west and north–south routes. No 160 (VH 6751), which ran until 1956, stands at the Kentwood Roundabout terminus — just short of Tilehurst railway station — in the days before the route was extended to Armour Hill. *Harry Luff / Online Transport Archive / Photobus*

The first examples from a 20-strong batch of new trolleybuses entered service in March 1949 — before the majority of the Karriers, hence the number range 138-57. The newcomers featured 56-seater bodywork by RCT's trusted supplier, Park Royal, mounted upon British United Traction chassis — all but one fitted with English Electric equipment. The odd one out was No 154, which had Metro-Vick electrical equipment from new. No 144, photographed before entering service, was also destined to be the formal 'last trolleybus' to run in Reading, in 1968. *Colin Morris collection*

Apart from being the last of Reading's new trolleybuses to be fitted with small blue lights above the front destination aperture, the BUT 9611T type introduced several novel features to the RCT fleet. First, the platform was enclosed by power-operated doors. The initial step up was narrow, and the left of the platform and the lower saloon floor were on the same level. Secondly, the vehicles were a spacious 8ft wide. To conform with Ministry of Transport safety rules, a hand-operated emergency door was incorporated in the rear framework. *Ian Allan Library*

Carefully driven by a trainee driver, with an instructor seated in the cab behind the 'L' sign, BUT 9611T trolleybus No 138 (DRD 138), the first of its 1949 batch, had been relegated in the autumn of its career to tuition-vehicle status. The vehicle is travelling south-east toward the terminus and turning-circle at the Three Tuns inn, Wokingham Road. It is passing a well-patronised Palmer Park, which had lost its once extensive run of ornate wrought-iron railings in the 1940 munitions drive. *Brian Deans / D. E. Wall collection*

From 1950 all RCT trolleybuses — not to mention motor buses — were fitted with power-operated doors. As a result the incidence of passengers' being hurt whilst attempting to board or alight from a moving vehicle dropped dramatically . . . which was just as well, for the 1950 batch of 12 Sunbeam S7/BTH/Park Royal trolleybuses could seat 68 passengers and accommodate a further eight standing. In size — and impact — they were the equivalent of the Brill-bogied tramcars introduced some 46 years previously. Sunbeam No 178 (ERD 149) demonstrates. *Photomatic / D. E. Wall collection*

Phase 2 of very long vehicles on the 'main line' route: No 174 (ERD 145), a Sunbeam S7/ Park Royal trolleybus seating 68 (two fewer than the long-departed bogie trams) heads west towards Tilehurst in the 'Fifties, seeming to span the width of St Mary's Butts and block out the light as it crosses West Street Junction. At this crossing particularly, the wires hissed and the trolley-heads clacked through the points, sending a spitting display of blue sparks downward, whilst that heavy web of overhead bounced in protest. The buses themselves were silent enough, but . . . *D. E. Wall collection*

Someone must have nipped rather smartly along Oxford Road to catch Sunbeam S7 No 174 (ERD 145) passing the site of the old Reading Tramways Co depot and squeezing gently beneath the replacement metal version of the Reading West railway bridge, during which manœuvre the trolley poles lay practically parallel to the vehicle's roof. The notorious water-retentive dip in the road is still in evidence, but the drains have been improved somewhat. The now-famous route number 17 (and the others) appeared in 1964. *D. E. Wall collection*

The three-axle Sunbeam S7-type trolleybuses were intended primarily to cope with the heavy traffic on the main east–west routes but in the event were equally to be seen running to the two points south, from Caversham Bridge and Reading Stations. Operating on route 17 over the 'main line' from Wokingham Road to Tilehurst, No 170 (ERD 141) makes the wires hiss just to the west of the Gaumont Cinema — a good source of evening custom in those days — in Oxford Road. *D. E. Wall collection*

Heading east and looming large ▲
in Broad Street, Sunbeam S7/
Park Royal 68-seater No 180
(ERD 151) cruises past a none-
too-steady jay-walker —
anticipating by a few decades
the pedestrianisation of this
stretch — and a parked car, the
latter reflecting in its windscreen
a somewhat decorative image of
the electrical overhead. As with
most (but not all) types of
trolleybus, there is a door on the
nearside of the cab — a feature
much appreciated by conductors,
who could join the driver for a
sandwich at the terminus.
D. E. Wall collection

▲ Part of the postwar housing
boom in Reading involved a
considerable amount of building
in the wider Tilehurst area.
In a swathe parallel to
Kentwood Hill and beside
Armour Hill there were
considered to be sufficient new
potential passengers to justify
an extension from the previous
terminus at Kentwood
Roundabout, and in the summer
of 1958 new overhead was
installed up the steep lower
section of Kentwood Hill to a
new turning-circle and lay-by
at Armour Hill. BUT No 154
and Sunbeam S7 No 178
take a rest on 8 May 1960.
John H. Meredith

▲ By 1950 the Reading fleet of both trolley- and motor buses had grown to 104 vehicles.
The Council had recognised the need to establish a new depot two years before and
decided to erect additional premises in Bennet Road. Designed by the Borough
Surveyor, the main section involved the reconstruction and conversion of an aircraft
hangar, whilst the 3¹/₂-acre site could accommodate up to 80 vehicles, of both types.
The new facility became operational in 1952. *Ian Allan Library*

▲ The Sunbeam F4A trolleybuses were Reading's first (and last) with front entrances. They also introduced to the electrically powered fleet a livery in which the upper and lower cream bands were replaced by cream-painted window frames — a scheme first worn by Reading's double-deck motor buses in 1950. A relaxation of regulations nationally permitted the carriage of 68 seated passengers on just two axles. Here is No 191 again, this time in Wokingham Road on 5 June 1965. *Peter J. Relf / D. E. Wall collection*

▲ Reading's last new trolleybuses were delivered in 1961. At that time few citizens could have guessed that a mere seven years later they — and all other surviving trolleybuses in the town — would be withdrawn and the system superseded completely by motor buses. The final batch comprised 12 Sunbeam F4A models, bodied by Burlingham of Blackpool, supplier to RCT of motor-bus bodies since 1957. No 191 (VRD 191) pauses in St Mary's Butts *en route* from Stations to Northumberland Avenue. *D. E. Wall collection*

The other end! Sunbeam F4A No 182 (VRD 182) has come to a standstill a shade awkwardly in Broad Street on 30 June 1963. The cause was the front entrance featured on this batch. Passengers waiting at stop signs (attached to traction poles) were frequently in two minds as to which end of the bus they should approach. No destination indicator was provided at the rear of the Burlingham bodies, so a letter system was reintroduced (and lasted until August 1964), but one had to be slightly advanced in years to remember that 'A' meant Tilehurst — Three Tuns! *Peter J. Relf / D. E. Wall collection* ▶

Turning at the Tilehurst terminus in April 1968 is Sunbeam F4A No 192 (VRD 192), the penultimate numerically of 12 such vehicles delivered in 1961 and which proved to be the last new trolleybuses for Reading. The 68-seat bodywork was by Burlingham of Blackpool, No 192 being one of six equipped with 95hp BTH electrical equipment. *Mike Hodges*

The Reading Corporation trolleybus system at its greatest extent. Routes to Whitley Wood and Northumberland Avenue (beyond Whitley Street) started in 1949, the latter being extended to Whitley Wood Road in January 1963. The system closed piecemeal from January 1967, the last trolleybus running — on the 'main line' — on 3 November 1968. *Colin Morris*

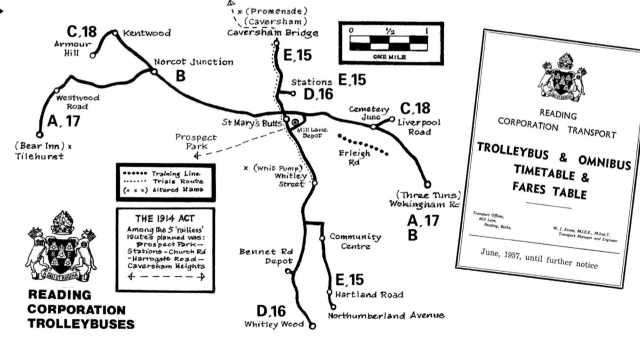

C,18 Kentwood
Armour Hill
x (Promenade) (Caversham)
Caversham Bridge
E,15

Norcot Junction
B
Stations E,15
D,16

Westwood Road
Cemetery Junc
C,18 Liverpool Road

A,17
St Mary's Butts
Mill Lane Depot

(Bear Inn) x Tilehurst
Prospect Park
Erleigh Rd

•••••• Training Line
...... Trials Route
(x x x) Altered Name
x (Whit Pump) Whitley Street
(Three Tuns) Wokingham Rd
A,17
B

THE 1914 ACT
Among the 5 'railless' routes planned was:
Prospect Park –
Stations – Church Rd
– Harrogate Road –
Caversham Heights
← – – – – – →

Community Centre

Bennet Rd Depot

E,15
Hartland Road

READING CORPORATION TROLLEYBUSES

D,16
Whitley Wood
Northumberland Avenue

0   ½   1
ONE MILE

READING CORPORATION TRANSPORT

TROLLEYBUS & OMNIBUS TIMETABLE & FARES TABLE

Transport Offices,
Mill Lane,
Reading, Berks.

W. J. Evans, M.I.E.E., M.Inst.T.
Transport Manager and Engineer

June, 1957, until further notice

Sunbeam F4A trolleybus No 187 (VRD 187) was one of six of its type fitted, prior to entering service, with 80hp English Electric equipment salvaged from withdrawn AEC trolleybuses; the five chosen by Tees-side Municipal Transport for further service following closure of the Reading system in November 1968 featured BTH equipment. *Mike Hodges*

Awaiting passengers for Wokingham Road, Sunbeam F4A No 192 (VRD 192) presents the somewhat austere rear aspect of this batch of trolleybuses. Photographed in 1968, the vehicle displays the famous 'main line' route number 17; until 1964 it would have shown the letter 'A'. *Mike Hodges*

In April 1968 Sunbeam F4A No 190 (VRD 190) and one of its fellows share the open expanse of Broad Street with 259 (KRD 259F), a recently delivered Bristol RELL6G/Strachans 'crush-loader' saloon and a type specifically intended to replace the trolleybuses by the end of the year. An RCT Traffic Regulator stands on duty behind No 190. *Mike Hodges*

Looking in very good condition (front number-plate aside), No 177 (ERD 148), a 1950 Sunbeam S7 with 68-seat Park Royal body, passes West Street junction and enters Broad Street on its journey east from Tilehurst to The Three Tuns, Wokingham Road. This vehicle would survive until two days before the ultimate closure of the trolleybus system on 3 November 1968. *Mike Hodges*

Sunbeam S7 No 177 waits beside the water-tower at Tilehurst — a location earlier relieved by large trees, which once graced the spot where now stands the row of shops (see page 41). Such a scene evokes feelings of nostalgia among transport enthusiasts, but few of today's environmentalists would care to have all those poles re-erected in their 'front yard'. *Mike Hodges*

'Drawing circles in the sky' — well, almost! Reading's Sunbeam S7 six-wheelers, with six-bay Park Royal bodywork, were handsome vehicles indeed and are much missed by local enthusiasts old enough to remember them — so much so that a slightly embarrassed model-maker has been persuaded to produce a replica which calls for rather more imagination than is usually required. *Mike Hodges*

After the last of the MMC wagonettes (1903) had been driven off the Caversham Road by the laying of tram lines, no further motor buses were licensed to operate from a base in Reading for over a decade. Between January and July 1913 a local syndicate tried, without success, to establish services to Caversham, Emmer Green, Sonning Common, Shiplake and Henley. (Curiously, the group submitted two photographs of a Kent-registered Maltby charabanc as an example of what it intended to run.) Permission was also refused that October for G. L. Hayward of Spencers Wood; he took four bus-loads per weekday into town, but could take out only those passengers he had earlier brought in.

The Council was keeping its options open as to what form of passenger transport it should adopt, for the 1913/14 estimates included £3,500 for motor buses. Among the schemes proposed were motor-bus services between Caversham Bridge and Harrogate Road, between the Railway Stations and Prospect Park, between Oxford Road tramway terminus and Tilehurst and between Caversham Heights and Tilehurst, the return route via St Anne's Road, Priest Hill, The Mount and Albert Road.

As with the tentative scheme for trackless trolleys, World War 1 set the Council back on its heels. However, even if, as a result, the Council could not raise the funds to go ahead at that time, it was obliged to acknowledge that troops and munitions workers needed to move about the area in increasing numbers, so on 19 July 1915 the British Automobile Traction Co Ltd — which firm set up its local headquarters at 113/115 Caversham Road — was sent its first 5s (25p) licence for a (Leyland) motor bus based in Reading. Thus came to Reading the branch of BAT which became the Thames Valley Traction Co Ltd. In preparation, BAT had already (21 December 1914) made provision for the protection of Reading Tramways (by a minimum fare structure), and a joint parcel scheme, worked out with Corporation officials, came into being in January 1916. In that month the Aldershot & District Traction Co Ltd was granted five licences to run between the Stations and Aldershot (jointly with BAT), and joined the Corporation parcel scheme. So, as far as motor buses are concerned, the forebears of First Beeline were there first.

Following the Armistice — and the return of sufficient demobilised men to crew vehicles and maintain them — the Tramways Committee members weighed up their options. Further consideration of trackless trolleys was shelved in favour of what they had experienced in their very own streets — motor buses.

During Reading's deliberations in 1913 over what kind of transport to employ, Thornycroft — in hope — sent a double-deck demonstrator to the town. The following year Daimler, Dennis, Straker-Squire and Tilling-Stevens all tried their luck, the last sending across from Maidstone KT 610, its already well-travelled petrol-electric demonstrator. Reading did not choose any of them.
Alan Lambert collection

On 24 March 1919 the Tramways Committee listened to George Craven's report and recommended that five motor buses, a shed (to be erected by direct labour at the tramway depot) and everything else necessary for setting up a motor-bus service be provided, the cost — £7,750 (of which the shed amounted to £450) — to be defrayed out of the Rescue Fund.

A facility was duly established at Mill Lane for building the double-deck bodywork for the first two AEC YC chassis. No 1 (DP 2362) was first sent out on familiarisation runs without a windscreen and painted flat grey, with just the letters 'RCT' over the rear wheel arches. On Wednesday 15 October 1919 members of the Tramways Committee sat on the open upper deck throughout the trial from Caversham Heights to the Plough Inn, Tilehurst, via Norcot Road, pencilling into their notebooks where the trees needed trimming, roads widening and Post Office wires raising.

Still without windscreens initially (well, those tough tram drivers hadn't got them), the first two AEC double-deckers, now in a blue-lined grey livery and lettered 'READING CORPORATION MOTORS', entered passenger service over the surveyed route on 6 December 1919. To avoid taking traffic away from the trams they went between Stations and the Oxford Road tram terminus by way of Castle Street, Bath Road, Liebenrood Road, Waverley Road and Grovelands Road. As the fleet grew, licences were granted to nine specially trained drivers and practically all the tram conductors. Fares were charged at '1d per mile or part thereof, with a minimum fare of 2d for and less distance than 2 miles'. George Craven was to write many years later: 'I am proud that I was able to inaugurate the motorbus in 1919.' However, it was James Calder (at a salary of £700 per annum upon his appointment as Manager and Engineer) who was to set up the new offspring of a suitably renamed Reading Corporation Tramways & Motors Department upon what would turn out to be its very long-lived feet. A second service, between the Star Inn, Lower Caversham and Shinfield Road via Caversham Bridge, the Stations, Sidmouth Road and Redlands Road, started on 3 July 1920.

The next two AEC YC chassis had bodies by outside contractors as 22-seat single-deckers. After the fifth YC chassis had been delivered and fitted with a double-deck body at the Mill Lane works, a sixth, reconstructed chassis was bought from AEC (for £877 10s 0d) and also received an 'in-house' open-top body, the cost of building the bodywork for each of these being some £650.

Calder was to lavish just as much care and attention upon his motor buses as he did upon the trams and trolleybuses. On the

maintenance side he adopted Allen & Simmonds patent pistons for the Tylor engines of the YCs, after experiments with No 1 from August 1920 disclosed an improved pulling power and an immediate cessation of exhaust smoke. It was estimated that over a period of seven weeks 67 gallons of lubricating oil had been saved — a considerable reduction in running costs — and all six buses delivered by the end of 1920 were refitted, at a total cost of £130. Despite such efforts to overcome the inefficiency of the Tylor engine, throughout the 'Twenties — as was the case with other municipalities — motor-bus services needed support from profits earned by the trams.

By the time the third bus service, from Emmer Green to Lower Whitley, had been established, in 1925, only eight more buses had been ordered — four more AEC YC (three double-deckers and a saloon), two Guy BA 20-seaters, a Guy B 26-seater and a Thornycroft JB 'London J' with 52-seat open-top double-deck bodywork built in-house by the Tramways & Motors Department and (according to Edgar Jordan) featuring a cab so small that there was at least one driver who couldn't squeeze himself into it. In the years 1926-9 the Corporation took delivery of eight Guy B saloons, four Guy CX 54-seat open-top double-deckers, two Karrier CL6 32-seaters, four Guy FCX 32-seaters (with the last

Reading Corporation's first motor bus was an AEC YC (DP 2362) with 46-seat bodywork built by its own workforce at Mill Lane. It was one of a pair which entered service in December 1919, and ran for some 8½ years — always on solid or NAP tyres. Edgar Jordan remembers that in their latter days, as the driver let in the clutch, they took off with a noise like a hiccupping turkey.
Alan Lambert collection

AEC YC Nos 3 and 4 originally carried 22-seat saloon bodywork, built by Baker & Jefferies in the winter of 1919/20. However, after just a few months RCT turned them both into 46-seat double-deckers, by simply adding a staircase and an upper deck, complete with seats, decency panels and railings. No 3 (DP 2364) is seen when newly rebuilt. *Alan Lambert collection*

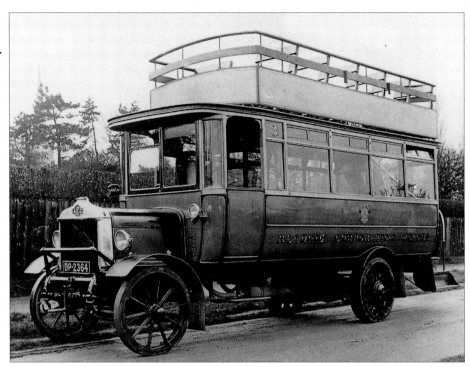

RCT fitters at Mill Lane work on a 1925 Guy BA 20-seat saloon bus, purchased to convey children from around the town to a special school in Northumberland Avenue, Whitley. The smallest vehicles in the fleet, Nos 11 and 12 (DP 6373/4) were fitted from new with pneumatic tyres and with driver-operated folding doors at the front. *Michael Plunkett collection*

No 19 (DP 7257) was one of seven Guy B saloons bodied by RCT in 1925/6. The batch featured several detail differences; on No 19 a Guy 'feathers in our cap' filler-cap adorned the radiator, and the coat of arms was encircled by a garter bearing the words 'Reading Corporation Motors'. Edgar Jordan recalls that these 26-seaters eventually developed noisy engines and became 'rattle-boxes'. *Alan Lambert collection*

Posing on the ferro-concrete Caversham Bridge, opened to traffic in 1926, is the Corporation's one-off Thornycroft JB, No 14 (DP 7016), with bodywork built by the Corporation. Thornycroft, based 'just down the road' at Basingstoke, must have had high hopes for repeat orders. Yet, despite being re-shod with pneumatic tyres, it was liked by neither drivers nor fitters, consequently spending much of its time in the far corner of the garage. Despite receiving repeat orders from Bournemouth, Southampton and Portsmouth, Thornycroft never sold another bus chassis to Reading.
Colin Morris

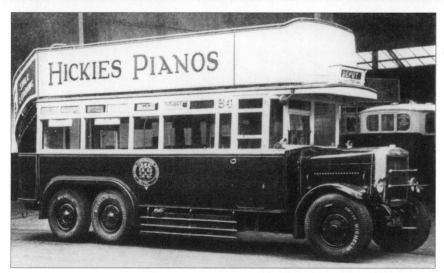

Magnum opus of the Mill Lane bodyshop in 1927 was the construction of 54-seat open-top bodywork for four three-axle Guy CX double-deckers. No 24 (DP 8751) is pictured new outside the East Garage in November 1927 before entering service. After some 3½ years in this form all four would undergo a radical and remarkable metamorphosis.
Alan Lambert collection

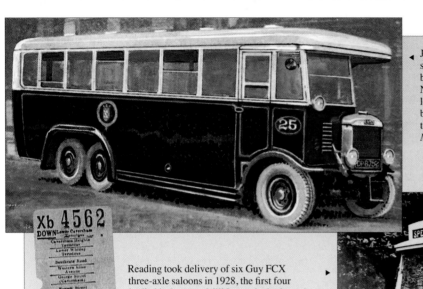

Just two Karrier CL6 three-axle saloons entered service in 1928, with 32-seat forward-entrance bodywork built at Mill Lane by the Corporation. No 25 (DP 8752) and sister vehicle No 26 lasted less than five years in the service of Reading, but their bodywork was retained and transferred to a pair of Guy FCX six-wheelers.
Michael Plunkett collection

Reading took delivery of six Guy FCX three-axle saloons in 1928, the first four bodied in-house at Mill Lane; the bodywork of the other two (Nos 31/2) was that replaced in 1933 by earlier RCT handiwork. Guy has been attributed blame for the inferior original bodies but, as the transfer (behind the door) on No 31 (DP 9712) reveals, 'hands up' Hall Lewis, forerunner of— Park Royal!
Michael Plunkett collection

The last five B types built by Guy for Reading also featured that firm's bodywork. These 25-seater saloons were delivered 1928-30. No 40 (RD 2114) and sister vehicle 41 had bodywork of a sophisticated style which probably convinced RCT that technological advances in bodybuilding were moving beyond its capabilities.
Michael Plunkett collection

complete bus bodies built in the Mill Lane workshop) and two Guy FCX 28-seaters with Hall Lewis bodywork.

Two further Guy B saloons, with 25-seat Guy bodywork, were purchased in 1930. These, however, were received after the first four examples of Leyland's revolutionary lowbridge TD1 Titan had been taken into stock, shortly to replace the trams on the Bath Road route. 'Buy a Titan and bury a tram' ran the unsweetened Leyland publicity at the time. A later example took this rather too literally, colliding with tram No 16 on the Oxford Road route in December 1936 and putting it out of action for some four months.

The second route upon which trams were replaced with buses was that along Erleigh Road, in August 1932, by which time a further seven Titans were available. For the same reason that all Reading's trams had been open-toppers, and its first six trolleybuses of lowbridge configuration (*i.e.* the presence of railway bridges with restricted headroom), these and all other new double-deckers for Reading continued what became a lowbridge double-deck tradition lasting until 1957. An exception was the batch of four Guy CX open-toppers, which in 1931 became 'highbridge' closed-top double-deckers, courtesy of the Corporation's bodyshop in Mill Lane. Built upon an already high chassis frame, the result was positively awkward-looking. Edgar Jordan recalls watching one from the platform of Reading West station as it passed over Tilehurst Road railway bridge some

400 yards to the south: 'It looked absolutely unsafe, towering so precariously; one had the impression that a strong wind could blow it off.' In this form the Guys were prohibited from the roads beneath the Vastern Road and Oxford Road railway bridges but could just squeeze under that in Caversham Road.

Having made its mark in Reading with its Titan TD1 model, Leyland Motors must have been considerably dismayed to learn that the town was to turn for future double-deckers to its rival, the Regent, a product of the Associated Equipment Co (AEC), upon which Reading was to rely for new bus chassis until 1965. Included among the World War 2 intake, two either side of the six

This Titan, No 3 (RD 3676), pictured outside the Mill Lane depot, was Reading's last, a TD1A delivered in 1932. It was an odd creature, in that the typical piano-fronted Leyland bodywork featured destination apertures, front and back, which had been dropped almost to cant-rail level. That at the rear was mounted in a distinctly 'pouted' housing. *Michael Plunkett collection*

▲ With complaining brake linings, No 22 (DP 8749) rolls to an early-morning stop at the Maypole Dairy on Broad Street's north side in 1932. This awkward-looking vehicle was one of the previously open-top Guy three-axle double-deckers, all having been fitted with covered tops by the Corporation the previous year. Already mounted on high-framed chassis, the buses were now of highbridge construction, which meant that the vehicles towered above the rest of the traffic in town. They were also unusual in that comparatively few enclosed-top double-deckers in Britain were of normal-control layout. *Colin Morris*

utility trolleybuses of 1943, were four equally austere Strachans-bodied Guy Arab double-deckers — again, of lowbridge configuration — which were to put in some six or seven years' service in Reading.

Whereas vehicle dispersal (parking vehicles at night anywhere but in the depot, so that one bomb could not destroy most of the fleet) was not practicable with trolleybuses, it certainly was with motor buses. Until the last year of the war, when British and American aircraft ruled the skies, they were placed out around the town, the wide, quiet stretch of Sidmouth Street seeming to attract a fair share.

In his fascinating article for *Buses and Trams* (1949) John Evans produced a comparative list of Reading's population against the growth of the municipal transport services. During the early part of World War 2 the population, swelled by evacuees, stood at 124,000; by 1944 (by which time many of the evacuees had gone home and members of the armed services had started visiting the Continent) the figure had fallen to 111,340, and the following year (of victory) it was 108,830. However, apart from a slight blip in 1944 (the year of the invasion of Normandy), the totals, in terms of mileage and numbers of passengers carried, continued to rise steadily, from 2,253,908 and 24,318,420 respectively in 1940 to 2,612,748 and 41,385,031 in 1945. These two figures continued to rise in the peace that followed, although in 1948 the population was still 100 short of the 114,600 who had lived within the Borough in 1940.

The figures, of course, relate to both trolleybuses and motor buses, but they do illustrate how, in a time of continuing motor-fuel rationing, the bus remained a good and cheap means of local travel. This was to remain the case until the Finance Act 1950 let slip the leash and, over the next two decades, persuaded many people that buying their own means of transport was a viable option. The effect, however, was greatest in the countryside surrounding Reading, and the result was the increasing vulnerability of the local territorial company, Thames Valley, rather than Reading Corporation Transport . . . which is the point

at which William John Evans' stubborn personality was brought to bear, laying the bedrock upon which future success was built. 'Redoubtable', he has been called; irritable, certainly — 'You do not need to address me when I am in the street', an employee was warned. However, according to Mike Russell (later to become Operations Director of Reading Transport), 'irrespective of what he was like . . . he was a very, very good transport manager . . . Reading Transport would not be here today had it not been for the way he steered the undertaking through 20 postwar years'. Tom Pruett, sent to Reading by the Tilling organisation to enable its subsidiary Thames Valley to overcome its difficulties, caused in large part by the fares protection granted to RCT by the Traffic Act 1930,(by the attempted establishment of a Brighton-style area transport agreement), met his match in Evans. Once again, that little red light had been put to good use. Mike Russell: 'I have seen the correspondence files; they are voluminous . . . very long, cogent arguments as to why this should or should not be done — he had the best of each and every one of the arguments . . .

In 1933 Reading re-established its patronage of AEC with the purchase of its first AEC Regent. No 4 (RD 4337) was a 661 model with six-cylinder A162 engine — one of just three in the fleet which ran on petrol. The angular six-bay bodywork, perforce still lowbridge, was RCT's first by Park Royal, if the earlier Hall Lewis saloons are discounted. *Michael Plunkett collection*

As a result, by 1957 Evans had engineered a situation whereby Thames Valley had to put up with RCT running beyond the Borough boundary to a significant extent . . . It proved to be the thin end of the wedge . . . From that point, Reading adopted the stratagem that the serving of the urban area which looked to Reading as its centre, irrespective of whether it was within the Borough or not, was a matter for Reading Corporation Transport.'

Such incursions continued piecemeal over the years until, in 1964, Reading suffered its one and only (slight) setback in this respect. Wishing to serve new developments to the west of Overdown Road and establish a route through Long Lane, RCT found itself opposed by a competing application from

Thames Valley. As Mike Russell relates, '. . . the Commissioner of the day sent the two parties away to sort themselves out and come back with a joint application. It became the only joint operation there ever was during the course of the separate existence of Thames Valley and Reading Corporation Transport.' It was an arrangement not much enjoyed by Reading, but it was to last some 11 years.

In the midst of his resolute consolidation of the traffic side of the undertaking, Evans the engineer was equally hard at work. Among the several innovations credited to him are the two for which he is best remembered — first, the introduction of platform doors on double-deck motor buses and trolleybuses and, secondly, the design and development of 'standee' single-deck

AEC toned things down a little for the 1935-8 deliveries of O661 Regents, which were fitted with the A172 six-cylinder engine of 7.58-litre capacity. Remarkably, No 47 (RD 7127) is still in existence, safe in the ownership of the British Trolleybus Society. It was delivered in August 1935 but lost its autovac three years later when converted to direct injection. *Daniel Hill*

Ordered at the same time (1933) as the first two Regents were a brace of AEC Regal 642 four-cylinder petrol-engined saloons with Park Royal bodywork. No 7 (RD 4340) and sister 6 featured the little white identification lights, carried by some — but not all — motor buses of the period, on each side of the front destination aperture. *Michael Plunkett collection*

Obliged, as were all other operators during World War 2, to purchase additional vehicles whence it could, RCT took delivery of its only Guy double-deckers. All four had wartime utility bodywork by Strachans. Nos 6 (BRD 754) and 7 of 1942 had Gardner 5LW engines, Nos 27 and 28 of 1943 being fitted with the larger 6LW unit. *Michael Plunkett collection*

With not much else available in 1946, William Little ordered six Bedford OB saloons with Duple bodywork. They served with RCT for just over two years. Evans had a further six bodied in virtually identical style by Mulliner, which lasted much longer. No 69 (CRD 592) was one of the latter and by virtue of a two-year interval with the Health Department was on strength until 1965. *K. C. Blacker / Michael Plunkett collection*

Park Royal must have been short of headlamps in 1947, for when the first AEC Regent II O661 double-deckers were delivered they lacked a nearside fitment. In February of that year No 60 (CRD 254) picks up a few eager passengers (for Shinfield Road) opposite The Angel at the eastern end of Broad Street — itself a stage-coach stop 100 years before. *Ian Allan Library*

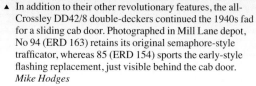

▲ In addition to their other revolutionary features, the all-Crossley DD42/8 double-deckers continued the 1940s fad for a sliding cab door. Photographed in Mill Lane depot, No 94 (ERD 163) retains its original semaphore-style trafficator, whereas 85 (ERD 154) sports the early-style flashing replacement, just visible behind the cab door. *Mike Hodges*

▲ Following his innovative 'trolleybuses with doors' John Evans ordered his first double-deck motor buses similarly fitted. Their registration numbers following on from the batch of Sunbeam S7 trolleybuses delivered at the same time (November 1950), they had chassis, engines and bodywork constructed by Crossley. No 86 (ERD 155) rests at Mill Lane in 1956. Similar No 85 survives in preservation. *D. F. Parker / Ian Allan Library*

Going home for the night, over long-disused tram rails, is 1950-vintage all-Crossley DD42/8 No 95 (ERD 164), the last numerically of a batch of 12. These were the first Reading motor buses fitted with platform doors, the first built to 8ft width and the first to feature route-number apertures. By the time this photograph was taken No 95's original semaphore-style trafficator had been replaced with a primitive 'flasher'. *Mike Hodges*

▲ A combination of generous front-corner pillars, large front wings, a narrow radiator and high-set headlamps gave the Crossleys a distinctly odd appearance. Equally distinctive was the Crossley-built bodywork, its rearmost lower-deck side windows echoing the sweeping curve of those on the upper deck. Reading's Crossleys weighed approximately a ton more than a contemporary AEC Regent. *Mike Hodges*

'Ker-lump!' Mind that door, Michael Russell is going to buy that vehicle! RCT's final batch of the AEC Regent/Park Royal combination, still with lowbridge bodywork, featured the Mk III 6812A version — five delivered in January 1956, four a year later. No 303 — ex 103, ex 3 — (MRD 146) is being dismissed in St Mary's Butts on 9 December 1976. *Colin Morris*

▲ No 96 (LDP 943), the first of nine AEC Regent IIIs delivered in 1956, exits Mill Lane in 1968 — before the 'squashed fly' RT logo was imposed upon the fleet. Bodywork was by Park Royal and seated 57. This type was the last to lowbridge configuration delivered to RCT, a more comfortable means of passing beneath the Vastern Road bridges arriving in 1962 with the Dennis Loline. *Mike Hodges*

John Evans' second motor-bus innovation for RCT was to prepare it for one-man-operation. With bodywork designed to his specification and built — to carry 34 seated and 26 'standee' passengers — by Burlingham, Duple and East Lancs, 32 such saloons entered service in Reading between 1957 and 1965, mounted upon AEC Reliance chassis. No 6 (NDP 424) of 1957 was Burlingham-bodied. *Ian Allan Library*

In one shot the highly observant photographer has managed to capture no fewer than three variations — Burlingham-bodied No 16 of 1959, East Lancs 47 of 1964 and Duple (Northern) 26 of 1962. Spot the detail differences! *Mike Hodges*

Turning out of Castle Street into St Mary's Butts *en route* from Grovelands is No 15 (SRD 15), a 1959 AEC Reliance 2MU3RV with Burlingham bodywork featuring a front entrance and centre exit; accommodation was provided for 34-seated passengers and some 26 'standees'. When H. V. Burlingham Ltd was taken over by Duple further examples were bodied under the latter's name, to be followed in turn by batches by East Lancs and Neepsend. *Mike Hodges*

AEC Reliance No 52 (CRD 152C) had an East Lancs body — one of four built at the Neepsend works in Sheffield. Withdrawn from service in 1979, the vehicle spent the best part of two years in retirement at the Bennet Road depot, until purchased by a unit of the Boys' Brigade. In 1989, however, it was acquired for preservation by Richard Rampton, in whose care it is seen here. *D. E. Wall*

motor buses best suited to the needs of a Reading already showing signs of traffic congestion. Never short of confidence, he also found time to explain these and other matters at some length in the journals of the trade press. He retired in July 1967.

With the exception of the early arrangement with Groves at the beginning of the 20th century, the top job at RCT had always been awarded to an electrical engineer. Now that trolleybuses were being dispensed with, the Council decided that it would be more appropriate to appoint someone who was by discipline a traffic man. Their very good choice fell upon Royston C. Jenkins, whose sound experience included time spent with the municipalities of Plymouth, Wigan, Rawtenstall and Middlesbrough. Whichever way things were going to pan out in the Government's forecast plans for the radical reform of local government, here was someone who'd seen how things were tackled elsewhere in sufficient variety to ensure the continuing good health of the Reading undertaking. The boundary-pushing exercise started by Evans was to be pursued with watchful and patient vigour.

Thames Valley, already beset with rapidly decreasing loading figures and staffing difficulties, was now positively ailing. However, the nationalisation in 1968 of the BET group's bus

Between September 1962 and December 1966 RCT took delivery of 26 examples of the Dennis Loline III based upon Bristol's Lodekka concept, with central gangway upstairs; Reading's double-deckers were still required to be of low height, as the Vastern Road railway bridges remained a problem. Originally numbered 35, No 135 (35 DP) of 1962 was, however, at work on the 'main line' ex-trolleybus route when photographed on 28 February 1976.
M.J.Russell

Undertaking a task for which the type was primarily purchased, Bristol RELL6G No 263 (KRD 263F), which entered service in January 1968, heads west on route 17, replacement for the 'main line' trolleybus service.
It was one of a batch of 14 with bodywork by Strachans, built at Hamble, near Southampton. Holding the centre line like a tram, it was photographed in Oxford Road in December 1976.
Colin Morris

Evening shadows lengthen as Bristol RELL6G No 258 (KRD 258F) departs from the Stations on trolleybus-replacement service 15 to Northumberland Avenue. Eight of these 'standee' saloons (34 seated, plus 35 standing) were available when this became the third trolleybus section to be abandoned, after service on 31 December 1967. Another RE and two Dennis Lolines are in attendance. *Mike Hodges*

'Nor bars a Reading Gaol make'! The ultimate crush-loader, 'standee' saloon — the interior (looking forward) of No 282 (NDP 282G), a Bristol RELL6G of 1968, with room for 34 seated passengers, plus 35 standing. The bodywork of this batch was by Pennine — and it rattled nicely, in memory of RCT's bodywork on its original Guy saloons of the 'Twenties. *Ian Allan Library*

interests had offered a temporary lifeline. In July 1971 Thomas Pruett had become a director of the Aldershot & District Traction Co Ltd and, on 20 December 1971 it was resolved that this company should be renamed as the Thames Valley & Aldershot Omnibus Co Ltd, reflecting its takeover of Thames Valley. The enlarged company proceeded to trade as 'Alder Valley' — a portmanteau name for a non-existent geographical feature; it must have seemed a good title at the time, but the paler shade of red it eventually adopted appeared to strengthen RCT's determination to gain ground wherever it made sense to do so.

The local-government reorganisation which became effective on 1 April 1974 looked at first likely to curb Reading's ambitions. The titles 'Corporation' and 'Alderman' were dispensed with, and thus the transport undertaking became plain 'Reading Transport'. Berkshire County Council, no doubt smarting at the transfer of a huge part of its territory to Oxfordshire, now sought to take a hand in the running of passenger transport in Reading; it considered that the long-established 'fares protection' enjoyed by Reading Transport was against the public interest and that the travelling public would have more buses to choose from if it were removed.

Map of Corporation bus routes c1970. *Colin Morris collection* ▶

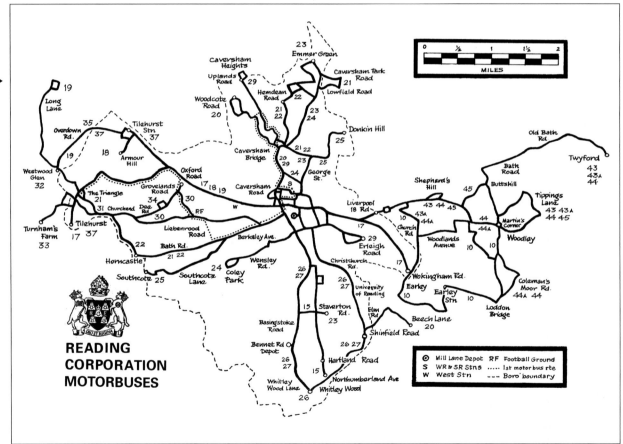

72

The 1971-4 deliveries of Bristol VRTLL6LX/Northern Counties dual-door 76- and 77-seaters perpetuated the long-established Reading tradition of low-height double-deckers — whichever way manufacturers achieved that end. The squat figure of No 53 (NRD 53M) of 1974 is emphasised by the comparative height of the Metropolitan bringing up the rear. *Colin Morris*

◄ From 15 November 1970 Broad Street was closed to all traffic save buses and service vehicles. This 1974 photograph emphasises the comparative freedom to wander, not enjoyed by pedestrians thereabouts for some 60 years. The bus is low-height Bristol VRTLL6LX No 59 (NRD 59M), *en route* to Tilehurst. *Ian Allan Library*

▲ Long-awaited adjustments to the clearance beneath the Vastern Road railway bridges meant that Reading could at last order (and receive) full-height double-deckers in quantity, which it proceeded to do in the summer of 1976. Northern Counties-bodied Bristol VRTLL3/6LXB No 40 (NDP 40R) heads west in Oxford Road that same year. *Colin Morris*

Bristol VRTLL/Northern Counties No 36 (NDP 36R) leaves St Mary's Butts for St Michael's, Tilehurst, on 9 December 1976.
The bus is decked out in a livery of pale blue, black and white to promote the £5 Reading Rover ticket, offering unlimited travel for a month. At the time the driver asked for a copy of this photograph; sorry it's taken so long!
Colin Morris

Unfortunately for Alder Valley, in addition to the problems it had inherited from Thames Valley, it now found great difficulty in recruiting sufficient fitting staff. As a result a great number of hired buses were brought in from all over Southern England; a service bus from Reading to Twyford — if it turned up at all — was quite likely to be a Royal Blue coach or Maidstone Borough Council double-decker. Mike Russell: 'This led to Berkshire County Council being besieged by complaints from the representatives of Woodley and from Wokingham District that the service was unreliable — and they wanted something done about it. A deal was struck whereby Reading agreed to give up protection within the Borough in exchange for a takeover of the routes to Woodley . . . part of that deal was that the joint service (19) to Long Lane became exclusive to Reading Transport, thus bringing about the end of that one-off joint-working agreement.'

The general concept from Reading Transport's viewpoint was to keep up the volume of business. This was the major theme throughout the Royston Jenkins years, 'that whatever had to be cut somewhere should be balanced by some compensatory advantage somewhere else; in effect, by pushing forward into other swathes of territory when existing business was starting to fall away. There was a lot of new development, either taking place or scheduled to take place in the area immediately outside the Borough of Reading — and Reading wanted to serve it . . . It led to a series of Traffic Court battles with Alder Valley, [most of] which were effectively decided in Reading's favour . . . Reading was in a stronger position to put in a better and more attractive level of service for each new development than Alder Valley, whose offering was generally a diversion of an existing service . . . we expanded to Ford's Farm, Calcot, Beansheaf and to Purley [1983]; and then in the other direction we expanded further in Woodley as the Airfield development got underway . . . We started going to Lower Earley with a token service in 1979 . . . and in 1983 a full service was put in.'

Not surprisingly, by 1980 Reading Transport's management had discussed at fairly frequent intervals 'What are we going to do if the phone rings one night to say that Alder Valley has gone bust? — we worked up a proposal to take over all bus operations in the Greater Reading area and, if necessary, to establish interchange points with long-distance routes at the fringes: but it didn't!' It seems that such a plan would have involved an extra 22 vehicles. There was also some concern about the western fringes if Alder Valley should leave the Newbury area unserved, to be taken up perhaps by a vigorous newcomer. This led to discussion,

not too deep, with Thamesdown (formerly Swindon Corporation) Transport, which was equally aware of the problems which might develop from such a situation. Both parties concluded at that stage that they should take no action.

Royston Jenkins' unwritten motto during these stirring times was 'We shall be judged upon our record'. A plaudit which perhaps helps sum up that record is that, after a consolidation and tidying-up exercise which took account of changes resulting from an eventual deal with Alder Valley, together with substantial change in town services, a timetable was issued on 1 April 1985. Four years later, a transport officer who had worked elsewhere in the industry remarked that 'it was a wonderful tribute to Reading that in 1989 one could still pick up an April 1985 Reading bus timetable and discover that, effectively, it was still in force'.

Earlier, in 1980, the deregulation of express-coach services had been seized upon by Reading Transport in no uncertain manner; Alder Valley's Londonlink services came under threat also. Ignoring a comparatively brief attempt by Smith's Coaches of Reading to take advantage of the new legislation, Royston Jenkins had seen the desirability of establishing a coaching arm and to 'run trips to London'. During the run-up to this particular 'D-Day', at a meeting of municipal transport officers, Mike Russell had met a fellow traffic manager, Derek Giles of Southend Transport, who told him: 'We are thinking of running a coach service to London and on to Heathrow Airport.' Initially as a joke,

En route from Woodcote Road, Caversham, to Beech Lane via Kendrick Road and Shinfield Road, No 102 (ORD 102R), a Scania BR111DH / MCW Metropolitan of 1977, mounts the northern end of Caversham Bridge. The dual-door bodywork offered seats for 71 passengers and room for a further 12 standing. *Colin Morris*

The 1982 work-to-rule and go-slow on the competing railway boosted traffic considerably on the X1 Reading–London–Southend service, and additional journeys were introduced. MCW Metrobuses 159 and 165 prepare to set off in opposite directions from the London (Aldgate) pick-up and set-down point. *Richard Delahoy*

Scurrying past the Wellington Monument on London's Constitution Hill is No 182 (HCF 182W), a 72-seat MCW Metrobus on Reading–London–Southend route X1, worked jointly with Southend Transport. The photograph was taken in August 1981, soon after the bus had been delivered; both participants later curtailed their journeys to terminate in London, Reading Transport experiencing a 500% increase in traffic. *Colin Morris*

Russell replied: 'Well, if you're going to Heathrow, you might as well come on through to Reading, and we'll run it jointly.' Words spoken in jest were put to the respective managements — and joint service X1, running eight times a day, seven days a week between Reading and Southend, duly started on Deregulation Day, 6 October 1980. With the permission of London Transport, Aldgate was utilised as a picking-up and setting-down point; this facility stemmed from a meeting which the two traffic managers had with LT officials at 55 Broadway, London. A charming tailpiece attached to that is worth recording. The people they had met circulated a memo to all who might have an interest in the matter; it was formal, setting out what was proposed and asking for comments, but at the bottom was a hand-written postscript — 'PS: These people did not have to come and see us, but they chose to do so. Please help if you can!'

Coinciding with the introduction of the X1, Alder Valley withdrew its existing X12 service and started a new one which went straight to the M4 and on to London direct. RT initially went via the A4 — Twyford, Maidenhead, Slough, Heathrow — but by February 1981 had decided that its service should join the M4 at Maidenhead Thicket. It was the right decision; as Mike Russell

observed, 'The mileage was effectively identical to Alder Valley's quicker route, but there were no chimney pots along the motorway, so it was sound business.' After 15 months, however, it became apparent that the basic philosophies of the two municipalities differed; the two thus came to a friendly agreement to curtail their journeys at London and Heathrow, and the same kindly gentlemen at LT gave Reading their permission to use Aldgate as the London terminus.

Aided no doubt by a union-called work-to-rule and go-slow on the competing Reading–Paddington railway line, by 1984 the X1 service 'was so popular that it had gone up from the five buses we were running in 1982 to a maximum peak-hour 15 . . . and it was really busy . . . the buses coming out of London were jam-full. The best period for the X1 was 1983-6. We purchased specialist double-deckers for the service, and the Goldline image was designed together with an advertising agency on Castle Hill. Goldline was also used as the brand-name for the coaching activities from 1983 onward, in addition to the other regular express services like the ones to Birmingham and to Bournemouth via Winchester. We did very well on the latter in particular. For the first two or three years it was very popular.'

MCW Metrobus Mk II No 145 (A145 AMO), in full Goldline livery, cruises past the Granada cinema at The Lansdowne, Bournemouth — Yellow Buses territory — on 12 July 1986. From 1983 the Goldline brand had been expanded to cover other coaching activities, hence its use on (among others) the highly popular X2 Bournemouth service. *D. E. Wall*

Awaiting the 'off' at Reading Stations is Leyland Titan No 78 (RMO 78Y), one of five delivered in March 1983 to single-door layout and with 66 semi-coach seats; intended specifically for the X1 service, they had a top speed of 70mph and gave an excellent ride. It was envisaged that they would be converted to dual-door layout when relegated to bus work. *Colin Morris*

A further five Titans delivered in 1983 were rather more placid creatures; designed from the outset as stage-carriage vehicles, they had dual doors and bus seating for 70. In Broad Street, No 73 (RMO 73Y) picks up passengers for Northumberland Avenue as a typically attractive young citizen of Reading advertises her forthcoming status. *Colin Morris*

▲ The last dedicated vehicles for the Goldline X1 service were eight Leyland Olympian 64-seaters delivered in 1986/8. ECW-bodied No 83 (D83 UTF) swings out of Haymarket into Pall Mall East, just ¾ mile from its terminus. In its heyday the London service was highly successful, with a maximum peak-hour provision of 15 vehicles leaving London, with every seat filled. *Daniel Hill*

◄ Parked in a reflective Liverpudlian puddle is one of four Leyland Tiger/Plaxton Paramount 3200 coaches which were Royston Jenkins' pride and joy. The elegant Goldline livery was designed in Reading by Ray Murray & Partners. No 202 (RMO 202Y) had headed north in June 1984 with a party visiting the Liverpool Garden Festival. *Colin Morris*

Although new in 1978, Scania/MCW Metropolitan No 133 (SGM 133S) displays the style of livery in use at the time of the establishment of the 'arm's-length' municipally owned limited company. Gone is the RT 'squashed fly' logo, to be replaced with a far more dignified lower-case version of 'Reading Transport'.
D. E. Wall

The Tramways Act 1870 not only gave entrepreneurial groups opportunities to set up tramway systems; it also gave local municipalities powers eventually to purchase them. Thus the first provision for any kind of publicly owned transport was — perhaps unwittingly — enshrined in that Act.

Despite the fact that 19th-century aldermen and councillors were, in the main, the more successful Tory businessmen and shopkeepers of the community, they were — certainly as far as Reading is concerned — motivated by a genuine (and unpaid) regard for their philanthropic, secular and brotherly duties toward the local populace. Add to that municipal pride, a degree of dignity, a desire to improve the standard of living, relieve the rates where possible, appoint the right people and encourage and support them in their work, get re-elected and — who knows? — one day have that ormolu chain of office hung about their shoulders . . . or, perhaps, go on to become an MP. Nothing objectionable about any of that. So far, so good.

On a century, and a countrywide reorganisation of local-government structures by Edward Heath's Conservative Government in 1974 put paid to some of the outward trappings of that local pride; but it was Margaret Thatcher's Government a decade later which set out determinedly to dismember and disperse public ownership of any stripe. Although in the case of road transport the National Bus Company was the main target, municipally owned undertakings also were now perceived as labyrinths where socialists and trade unions lurked.

The radical Transport Act 1985 included a section which dealt with municipalities operating their own bus services. It did not state that such work should be given up; rather that the undertaking would have to be put at 'arm's length' from its council, in order to open it up to private competition. Despite an earlier Tory landslide in Reading — and a resultant Conservative Chairman of the Transport Committee from 1983 — there was an immediate cross-party, tri-partite campaign against such a provision as soon as it was spelled out in the preceding Bill. Members of Parliament were lobbied and representations made about the damage which could be done to an established and successful municipal like Reading — the loss of the ability directly to subsidise operations, and the possibility that the network might be destabilised by predatory action on the radial routes, in particular.

The odd situation at Reading was that Tony Page, the Labour spokesman on transport — with a sympathetic Conservative chairman locally — was, from 1982 (when the great majority of councils running local transport were Labour-controlled) Chairman nationally of the Federation of Public Passenger Transport Employers, which represented all the municipals at that time. In meetings with Transport Minister Nicholas Ridley, who was determined to stub out any opposition to his Bill, Page was told 'You're not going to survive' and (as the minister searched the carpet on his hands and knees for a screw dropped 'accidentally' from his glasses) 'The rigours of the market-place will see you go bankrupt'. Pure *Yes Minister*!

In May 1986 Labour took control of Reading Council, and Tony Page became Chairman of the Transport Committee. Upon the by now mandatory formation of Reading Transport Ltd

(Company No 2004963) in October of that year, Tony Page became Chairman of the Board, with Royston Jenkins as the executive Managing Director. Among the other members were trade-union representative John Banning and Councillors Bunty Nash and (later) June Orton, along with Mike Russell, Operations Director. In contrast with the situation at some other municipalities, the maximum permitted number of councillors was appointed, so that 'arm's length' really meant 'as close a Council control as possible'. Not too much was to be done at Reading without the Council's approval.

In the latter years of the National Bus Company it had not been unknown for major decisions to be made outside the boardrooms of its subsidiaries. Something not too dissimilar happened at Reading. Tony Page: 'It was becoming apparent that we needed to be a bit more commercially savvy . . . Traffic figures were static, or dropping slightly . . . We were pretty much in line with the average outside London, so there would have been, on average, a loss of about 2 or 3% per year . . . We needed to change the management and bring in someone from the private sector.' In other words, against the national trend, Reading Transport should have been making a handsome profit. Accordingly, in 1990, councillors were persuaded that change was necessary. The Managing Director took early retirement after 23 years' service; appointed in his stead was Rod Wilson, previously a highly successful marketing director with Black & Decker. As was intended, he had no experience in the sphere of passenger transport, nor in the public sector. The latter was to prove something of a stumbling-block.

In the meantime, whilst the accountancy procedures were reviewed and streamlined by recently-appointed Finance Director James Carney, Wilson set about transforming the whole culture of employee relations and launching marketing initiatives. Like many an enthusiastic new broom he encountered a difficult substance to shift — Mike Russell, Operations Director. The latter was also obliged to leave but, not wishing to depart from a Reading to which he had become somewhat attached, openly gave notice that, should it become appropriate, he reserved the right to set up his own company and run in opposition to RT. To fill the vacancy, the Council appointed Colin Thompson, a charismatic Wearsider with a strong passenger-transport background from both the municipal and private sectors.

All roads leading into and out of Reading town centre had for decades been unassailable municipal-transport territory. The external predatory competition forecast by Ridley did not

Long deemed an inappropriate place for minibuses, Reading at last made a gesture towards such things in 1988. Even then it chose the long version of the MCW Metrorider for its first half-dozen examples. In March 1989 No 605 (E605 HTF) was at work between Norcot and Caversham Bridge, wearing newly introduced 'Goldrider' livery and logos. *D. E. Wall*

▲ A brand-new Scania K113CRB coach with Van Hool Alizée bodywork purchased in April 1989 for the Goldline X1 service to London. Among the refinements it brought to Reading Transport was a toilet compartment. A courier seat was also provided in addition to the 49 available for fare-paying passengers. In 1992 the vehicle would be re-registered as BUS 5X. *Scania (GB) Ltd*

Whilst the production rights of MCW products were being negotiated and transferred to Optare it became necessary for RT to make a stop-gap purchase, and two Mercedes-Benz 811D/ Optare StarRiders entered the fleet in 1989. They suffered gearbox problems, and were withdrawn in 1991. No 608 (F608 SDP), thus a rare bird, was caught on camera on 27 May 1989. *John Marsh*

Old bus (well, 10-and-a-bit years old), new livery. The 'broken' white has been replaced with cream, which has 'slipped down' a bit — less on the top and more at the bottom. MCW Metrobus No 163 (WRD 163T) of 1979 demonstrates the trial livery introduced in 1990 — and superseded the following year. The single-deck version had a maroon band above the windows. *D. E. Wall*

82

The paint had scarcely had time to dry on the new cream and maroon livery when, in March 1992, an MCW Metrobus appeared with cream replaced, once again, by white and bearing a new logo — 'Reading Buses' underlined, vehicle length, by a turquoise band. This livery stuck, and six Optare MetroRiders delivered that year were the first new buses to wear it. No 610 (J610 SJB) turns into busy West Street. *D. E. Wall*

One of 10 ex-London Buses MCW Metrobuses which spent a large part of 1991 still dressed in this Harrow Buses livery whilst in service with Reading Transport, No 464 (E464 SON) was going about its business, looking good but different, in May 1991. Five more were repainted into Reading livery before entering service. *D. E. Wall*

In 1991/2 Reading played an important part in the launch of the DAF DB250/Optare Spectra and continued to favour the type throughout the decade. No 707 (L707 LJM) of 1994 was the only one which required its motor-driven blinds to be set manually each time by the driver — as the screen demonstrates at the Station terminus. *D. E. Wall*

materialise, for there were much easier pickings elsewhere. Rod Wilson therefore seized the 'opportunity' to extend the undertaking's operational network farther out beyond the Borough boundaries and in all directions. The key to this treasure lay with Len Wright's Berks Bucks Bus Company — 'The Bee Line' — successor to (in reverse order) Alder Valley North, Alder Valley, Thames Valley and BAT. Wright had begun a process of selling it off piecemeal. First, in 1991, Reading Transport acquired The Bee Line's Reading–London service (the ex-Thames Valley service B, later Alder Valley's X12) and amalgamated it with RT's own X1, marketing the whole as 'The London Line'.

The following year RT purchased the 'Reading Rural' routes, reaching as far afield as Oxford, High Wycombe and Newbury. The last, long seen as a possible and potentially damaging base for a competitive newcomer to the area, focused Reading councillors' minds somewhat. Len Wright, not wishing to find himself left with a totally detached rump, chose to include in the

sale the network of services radiating from this ancient West Berkshire town. Rod Wilson and Tony Page discussed the matter, and the Reading authority duly gave its approval. Rather than impose the newly introduced Reading Buses logo (underlined in turquoise) upon the outpost, RT chose a similarly designed Newbury Buses fleetname (underlined in green). Thus Newbury became the long-discussed defensive acquisition.

Reading Transport had absorbed all The Bee Line's Reading services save Rail-Air (to/from Heathrow) and its Bracknell-based routes. RT would have liked also to acquire the ex-Alder Valley bus station near the railway station, but Wright would not part with it. Additionally during this period impressive coaching independent Horseman Coaches Ltd of Reading became the subject of an unsuccessful bid.

Then just as it looked as though some of the initiatives launched by Rod Wilson were about to move things forward, an unforeseen spanner was thrust into the works. Mike Russell had not been bluffing. With time to sit and think carefully about a system which had been set up to be well-nigh competition-proof, he had surfaced with a raft of ideas — a chess player who'd practised tentative paper-moves against his former self. If weakness there were in a competition-free one-man-operated transport system, it was surely the dwelling-time at bus stops. In the town centre on core trunk route 17, for instance, this accounted for more than 20% of the running time. The only way to improve the 'commercial speed' would be to employ conductors, and that meant buses ready-made for such an operation — AEC Routemasters. Secondly, areas not then covered could be served by linking sections of existing routes. These two basic selling-points formed the nucleus of a business plan which rustled up the necessary finance. The Greater Reading Omnibus Co Ltd was registered with four directors; a key appointment was Jeff Stoute, formerly an engineering manager with Reading Transport, who also had 20 years' experience of working on Routemasters in London. In all 44 such buses, of which 35 entered service at one time or another, were based in and around a garage in Cardiff Road, dressed in a smart livery of red and cream. An eventual network of six services, on, extending, or linking up existing RT routes, commenced operating as Reading Mainline in July 1994.

The Borough Council immediately put up a spirited counter-attack, based, by and large (it would appear), on tactics employed elsewhere by Stagecoach. However, an expected three-week skirmish turned into a protracted battle lasting one month short of

Launched in 1992, 'The London Line' resulted from an amalgamation of The Bee Line (ex Londonlink) brand — newly acquired by RT — with Reading's existing Goldline X1 service to Aldgate. Dressed in a triple-blue livery — the first departure from Reading's traditional maroon — Optare-bodied Leyland Olympian coach No 86 (F86 MJH) is on the re-branded route L1. *D. E. Wall*

Single-decker coaches also operated on service L1. No 252 (J799 KHD) was a DAF SB2700 with Van Hool Alizée bodywork purchased practically unused from a dealer in 1992. Its arrival in November of that year brought the single-deck contribution to The London Line to a dozen vehicles, some of which began their journeys to the capital from Newbury. *D. E. Wall*

In August 1992, under the management of Rod Wilson, Reading Transport acquired Len Wright's Bee Line operations in the vicinity of Reading and Newbury. With the Reading operation came the Kenavon Drive, Forbury, premises and a sizeable fleet of vehicles mature but of a type new to RT — the Leyland National. No 322 (TBL 166M), new in 1974 to Alder Valley, emerges from the works still, like its fellows, in The Bee Line's livery but bearing Reading Buses vinyls. *Daniel Hill*

Some of the Leyland Nationals acquired by Reading Transport from The Bee Line received the green stripe and logo for Newbury Buses, finding themselves in some cases in the not unfamiliar surroundings of Newbury's Market Street bus station. No 357 (NPJ 483R) is pictured at the Reading terminus of route 100 on 4 April 1995. *D. E. Wall*

four years. Tony Page: '. . . the impact of Mainline was to hit [our] profit slap-bang where it hurt, because he was taking penny for penny off our bottom line . . . The order of the day was retrenchment. That was not what Rod Wilson was there to do. He hadn't expected this . . . A period of retrenchment required somebody who knew the industry well . . . we had to spend even more time with the Council — and that's where we had to have clear lines of communication between the two.'

Operations Director Colin Thompson had, a few months before, been redesignated Deputy Managing Director; in March 1995 he was elevated to the top job. As had been the case exactly 100 years before, when Harrison's 'Favorite' took on the vehicles of the Reading Tramways Co, lowered fares attracted a large number of passengers. Colin Thompson: 'We were both getting positive results on loadings, but the combined cost graph was going through the roof . . . an 8% increase in passengers, 30% in costs.' On the personalities front the conflict remained reasonably civilised, however. As in the 17th century, when rival supporters of Royalists and Parliamentarians in Reading simply went to different pubs '. . . it was a bit Civil War-ish. Most of the people working for Mike had worked previously for us . . . I'd known him for many years before I came here . . . when we were still in competition, we agreed to keep a dialogue going . . . [and] to do a double-act — each putting our case — before a public meeting of the Thames Valley branch of the Chartered Institute of Transport, at The Griffin in Caversham . . . I'd prepared two openings to my

Getting away as smartly as possible, MCW Metrobus Mk II No 457 (E457 SON) prepares to head south on an ex-trolleybus route in April 1995. Because the rival RM of Reading Mainline had a conductor — and therefore a much shorter 'dwelling time' at bus stops — it had a distinct advantage over the standard pay-as-you-enter double-deckers of Reading Transport. *D. E. Wall*

Turning out of Queen Victoria Street into Broad Street in 1996 (before both were fully pedestrianised) is an earlier 814 — an MAN 11.190/Optare Vecta 40-seater. This type, which operated from both Reading and Newbury depots, featured an upright frontal profile, more commonly associated with Optare's double-deck bodywork. Formerly an Optare demonstrator, M957 VWY was acquired in 1995. *Daniel Hill*

speech, dependent upon whether I was going to speak first or second.' Colin Thompson lost the toss: 'Well, it's no surprise to find I'm running just behind Mike!'

The CIT meeting in Caversham was by all accounts great fun, a really lively night enjoyed by all those present, but things couldn't go on the way they were, and the evening proved to be a turning-point. For both sides the cost of competing was out of all proportion to the benefits, but the greater resources lay with the Council. In due course the latter made an offer to take over the assets and liabilities of Reading Mainline — it was presented as a merger — which was accepted with effect from 1 June 1998. As part of the deal the Routemasters were kept running, still in red and cream, for another two years, with Mike Russell as Mainline General Manager, after which he was appointed Risk Manager for Reading Transport Ltd. As Colin Thompson reflected in 2005: 'Here we are, all these years later on. He's now in a managerial capacity with us.'

Thus ended an entertaining but costly variation on a post-1985 period riddled nationally by cross-pollinated policies — an admixture of Tory privatisation and a socialist perception, perhaps, of professional dignity as elitism. Ironically what happened in Reading was not the direct doing of the late Mr Ridley; 'the best-laid schemes . . .'

As part of a major scheme to redevelop the town centre, plans were put in train to move Reading Transport from its traditional home in Mill Lane to new custom-built premises in Great Knollys Street. A plaque in the foyer of the new depot commemorates the official opening on 2 July 1998, when the great and the good gathered in the presence of Cllr Tony Page, Chairman of Reading Transport Ltd, as the Rt Hon Dr Gavin Strang MP, Minister for Transport, performed the honours. Here was a minister who didn't want to see Reading divested of its municipal bus service. All that is missing from the plaque is a little red light for Oxford Road and a green one for London.

Inevitably, the retrenchment procedure involved cuts. When The London Line was launched there had been journeys both to Victoria and to Aldgate, but the latter were subsequently reduced in frequency and were ultimately withdrawn altogether at weekends. Reading

An effective response to the Reading Mainline challenge was the adoption, ahead of the national trend, of low-floor buses, attractive to passengers at both ends of age range. No 921 (R921 SJH), an Optare Excel, is a fine example. By October 2004 some 67% of Reading Transport services were low-floor-operated, putting the company well in the vanguard of the changeover. *Daniel Hill*

Built in 1987, this Leyland DAF 95 recovery truck has more than earned its keep whilst with Reading Transport. Rugged and powerful, it has been put to good use dealing both with RT vehicles and with passenger or heavy-goods vehicles stranded within range of Reading. For this latter purpose it is part of the nominal Reading Transport Engineering subsidiary. It is seen in the company of No 143 (A143 AMO), an MCW Metrobus Mk II double-decker coach (dubbed 'Poppy')
Daniel Hill

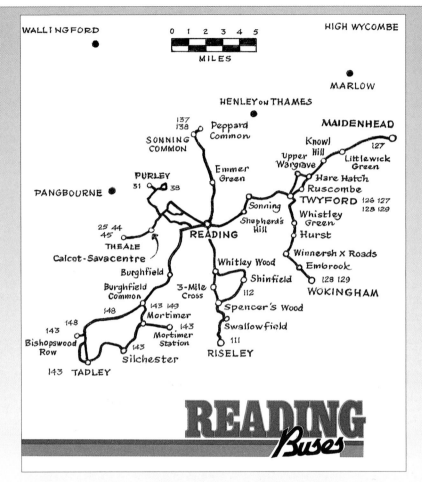

A 2005 composite route map of Reading Transport's 'Reading Rural' services. Although some routes have been integrated with those of the in-town services, most are as inherited from The Bee Line. Those towns indicated with a black disc are no longer served by RT; the erstwhile route to Pangbourne and Wallingford originally went all the way to Oxford upon acquisition in 1992. Silchester marks the position of Reading's Roman rival BC. *Colin Morris*

Transport persevered for as long as made sense, but The London Line seems to have been ailing from the outset. Increasing congestion on the M4 (leading to decreasing reliability in time-keeping), a slump in middle-management and senior clerical jobs in London during the early 'Nineties and an improved and more competitive rail service from Reading all combined to reduce patronage for coaches — and led to increasing discussion about the efficacy of The London Line. The operation was withdrawn in May 1999. Meanwhile most of the ex-Bee Line 'Reading Rural' services were integrated into the town network, whilst the northbound corridor were drawn back, to be run by other operators.

The western network, which became Newbury Buses, is still run as a separately named but integral part of Reading Transport Ltd. It speaks volumes for the company that an area which Red & White was quite happy to relinquish to Thames Valley (via the British Transport Commission) in 1950 — and one where the 'bus habit' practically died in the early 'Sixties because of high levels of car ownership — continues to be provided with a good range of stage-carriage services, centred upon Newbury bus station. Although only three West Berkshire County Council school contracts are operated at present, 40% of Newbury Buses passengers are children — getting the 'bus habit', one hopes.

Goldline, which originated with Royston Jenkins's desire to 'go coaching' in 1982, is today a major provider of revenue for Reading Transport. A semi-autonomous unit, with separate livery and dedicated staff, it has 11 coaches and a mini-coach, based at Great Knollys Street. Now exclusively a private-hire and coaching arm, it currently sees a turnover of some £¾ million per annum. The Goldline excursions programme includes UK destinations like Bournemouth and Blackpool — and trips to Disneyland in France.

A recent initiative has been to adopt the notion of 'positive rebranding'. Nine core routes have been identified. Only buses in special liveries are to be employed. The first brand was for the famous route 17, upon which the impressive Scania/East Lancs OmniDekka 90-seaters entered service on 25 October 2004 in a purple-based livery — a variation of a scheme devised by well-known commercial designer Ray Stenning. What the operator calls the 'generic' (or unbranded) version is a charcoal-based livery, so impressive that Colin Thompson has received a letter stating: 'It is the most beautiful bus I've ever seen'.

Next to be launched, in March 2005, were branded (dark green) routes 4, 5 and 6, for Worton Grange, Northumberland

Avenue and Whitley Wood in south Reading, using vehicles dedicated from a new batch of 12 Wright-bodied Scania single-deckers. The Council has invested some £2 million in new support equipment: new-style publicity, new shelters, real-time passenger information, plasma screens (which announce the next stop or the next bus due) and facilities to find that information by phone or personal desktop workstation. In the control room, inspectors can see the location of each bus, down to within 10ft — not unique, but well to the forefront of modern technology.

Forced into a few overloaded corridors by the courses of local rivers, Reading's motor traffic is heavy at the best of times upon roads which, as a result, need frequent attention. In the so-called rush-hour, when car drivers often observe traffic regulations in the breach, to gain half a mile in 40 minutes is considered good progress. In the midst of this, Reading's bus drivers set a high standard of concentration and care, which other road users would do well to emulate. I take my hat off to them. Well aware of the difficulties, the management strives to design rotas to fit the needs of individual drivers, allotting time shifts accordingly on differing pay rates.

As I bring these lines to a close, there comes the surprising news that Liberal Democrat-controlled Bournemouth Council is to sell its transport undertaking. (Don't they like the colour yellow?) One more municipal down; there's a moral there somewhere. When I first had the pleasure of meeting Colin Thompson I remarked that it is my wont, where appropriate, to bring my 'Glory Days' scripts up to the present. He was quick to respond: 'and as far as Reading is concerned, on into the future!' A very positive and reassuring note upon which to conclude.

Composite route map of the stage-carriage services operated in 2005 by Newbury Buses, trading name of the Newbury-based division of Reading Transport Ltd. The routes are basically those inherited from The Bee Line, tailored to meet current needs. Three routes maintain a physical link with Reading, and a further two with RT at Calcot. An earlier account of bus services in the area can be found in the work of Paul Lacey (details of which appear on page 96). *Colin Morris*

Reading Transport's first Optare Solo midibuses were ordered in 1998. Launched under the 'Here comes the Solo-Rider' banner, and continuing the 'Easy access for all' theme, the first entered service in Reading. Later examples included a similar Solo fleet for Newbury. Accordingly No 108 (V108 DCF) displays its green — rather than Reading's turquoise — bits. *D. E. Wall*

Long a borough council which is pro public transport, Reading is always looking to make things better. The Loddon Bridge Park & Ride scheme is a particularly successful example, launched with a signal-controlled priority bus lane (which made its passengers smug as they sailed past the otherwise static traffic). Optare Excel No 912 (P912 GJM) is in Loddon Bridge livery. *D. E. Wall*

In reflective mood: the last trace of an old rival's fleetname comes swinging out of High Street into King Street. Optare Excel 2 No 962 (X962 BPA), one of a quartet operated in a dedicated white livery under the Goldline banner for the Thames Valley Park shuttle service, was *en route* to that business park in November 2004. *Colin Morris*

At the Madejski Stadium, home of high-flying Reading FC — and the London Irish RFC — evening shadows point toward the daily change of role for a Day Track/Night Track Optare Spectra in September 2004. No 737 (YG02 FWA) has just delivered a homeward-bound collection of car-owners to the Park & Ride facility, on the Council-sponsored limited-stop Stations–St Mary's Butts–Green Park route, driven by a personable lady from Doncaster. This part of their work done, these vehicles are re-rostered to a series of 12 Night Track services operated between 8pm and 4.45am. *Colin Morris*

93

The newly acquired rural routes initially included a service which ran along the scenic A329 Thames Valley road all the way to Oxford. It was run by ex-Bee Line Leyland Nationals repainted in Reading's colours. Not enough people wished to admire the views, however, and the route was cut back to Wallingford. At Reading station on 4 April 1995 Leyland National 1151/1R No 314 (NRD 155M) awaits passengers for a 105 journey to Wallingford. That operation was not too remunerative either, and the service was later shortened again, to Pangbourne.
D. E. Wall

Newbury Buses operates a goodly number of the company's 'SoloRider' fleet of Optare Solo midibuses. No 118 (W118 SRX) departs Newbury on an early-morning run to Lambourn on service 4, which operates two-hourly, Mondays to Saturdays. In September 2003 No 118 suffered the indignity of being shunted off the road when hit from behind by a lorry — but has since recovered!
Reading Transport

In addition to an Optare Solo painted in a special green/blue/red livery (in 2002) for the workforce of the Greenham Common Trust, several Newbury buses have been dedicated for staff travel to the impressive Vodafone campus to the north of the town. These have included Solos, Excels and most recently a quartet of TransBus Enviro 300 saloons, including No 970 (KV03 ZGK).
Reading Transport

Following an impressive launch on Monday 25 October 2004 the first of a series of branded routes began operating in Reading. Not surprisingly, the long-established 'main line' route 17 was selected. Bringing a touch of gaiety to the Reading scene is Scania N94/East Lancs OmniDekka 814 (YN54 AFO) dressed in 'episcopal purple'. *Colin Morris*

Publicity material for the re-branded 17 route includes easy-to-read timetable leaflets and —emphasising the availability of information via personal computer — a route map in the form of a mouse mat.

BIBLIOGRAPHY

Three of the five lowbridge AEC Regent III/Park Royal double-deckers which entered service in January 1956 — Nos 96-100 — take a rest at Mill Lane in April 1974. The following year these vehicles would have 100 added to their fleet numbers, remaining thus for the rest of their employment with RCT. No 98 (LDP 945) was subsequently preserved in the ownership of Michael Dare, a founder member of the Reading (now British) Trolleybus Society, who sadly died shortly before this book went to press. *Colin Morris*

▼ Among the sources I have found helpful and/or recommend for further reading are:

Books

Hall, David A.: *Reading Trolleybuses* (Trolleybooks, 1991)
Hall, David A.: *Reading Trolleybuses* (Middleton Press, 1997)
Jordan, H. Edgar: *The Tramways of Reading* (Light Railway Transport League, 1957; Gordon, 1990)
Jordan, H. Edgar: *Reading Tramways* (Middleton Press, 1996)
Lacey, Paul: *A History of Newbury & District Motor Services Ltd* (Paul Lacey, 1987)
Lacey, Paul: *A History of the Thames Valley Traction Co Ltd, 1920-1930* (Paul Lacey, 1995)
Lacey, Paul: *Thackray's Way — a family in Road Transport* (Paul Lacey, 2001)
Lacey, Paul: *A History of the Thames Valley Traction Co Ltd, 1931-1945* (Paul Lacey, 2003)
Mountfield, David: *The Coaching Age* (Hale, 1976)
Wilson, Reg: *Municipal Buses in Colour, 1959-1974* (Ian Allan, 1997)

Booklets

Reading Transport 1901-1976 — 75th Anniversary (Reading Transport, 1976)
Stone, Graham L.: *Reading's Historic Buses* (Reading Heritage Travel, 1993)
Stone, Graham L.: *Buses of Reading and Newbury* (Reading Bus Preservation Group, 1994)

Journals and Magazine Articles

Bus Fare, monthly journal of the Reading Area Group of the British Trolleybus Society
Anon 'From Aircraft Hangar to Fully Equipped Garage', *Transport World*, June 1952
Boyle, Tom: 'Magnificent Men in Flying Machines' and 'Berkshire Old and Royal', *Reading Evening Post*, 1974
Calder, J. M.: 'Changing Over', *Bus & Coach*, July 1939
Evans, W. J.: 'Progress in Municipal Transport', *Buses and Trams* (Ian Allan, 1949)
Evans, W. J.: 'Why Reading uses Trolleybuses', *Public Transport*, May 1953
Evans, W. J.: 'What Price Doors?' *Bus & Coach*, February 1955
Evans, W. J.: 'Standee Operations at Reading', *The Transport Journal*, April 1959
Jordan, H. Edgar: 'Iron Wheel on Iron Rails', 'The Horses were a Ribby Lot', 'Free Rides on the Trolleys' and 'The All-Conquering Motor Bus', articles in 'Veterans of the Road — 75th Anniversary', *Reading Evening Post*, 1976
Russell, M. J.: 'Reading Transport: 75 Years of Progress', *Buses Extra* No 1 (Ian Allan, 1977)
Wise, Graham: 'Reading Transport', *Buses Extra* No 67 (Ian Allan, 1990)

Papers

Jenkins, R. C.: 'Some notes of Bus Priority Schemes in Reading' (RCT, 1970)

For those interested, a perusal of the relative traffic returns — in particular the number of passengers carried per annum — would shine an additional light upon the undertaking's affairs post Transport Act 1985.